NAMATJIRA

Wanderer Between Two Worlds

V. G. Chapman,
73 Stephen Dr.,
Woonona, 2517.

V. G. & R. S. CHAPMAN
73 Stephen Drive,
Woonona 2517
Ph. 84 2072

FRONTISPIECE

*Albert Namatjira, from a portrait
by Reg Campbell, reproduced by the
kind permission of the artist*

NAMATJIRA

Wanderer Between Two Worlds

JOYCE D. BATTY

With a Foreword by
SIR PAUL HASLUCK,
Minister for Territories 1951–1963

seal books
RIGBY

Cover photograph from the collection of the late Pastor S. O. Gross, and reproduced with the permission of Mrs E. Gross.

Rigby Limited, Adelaide • Sydney • Melbourne • Brisbane • Perth

First published in 1963 by Hodder and Stoughton Ltd.
Published in Seal Books 1976
Reprinted 1977
Copyright © 1963 by Joyce D. Batty
National Library of Australia Card Number
& ISBN 0 7270 0044 6

Printed in Hong Kong

For my sons
Ian and Christopher

FOREWORD

by Sir Paul Hasluck,
Minister for Territories 1951–1963

IN this book the author has been sedulous in bringing together from many different sources information about Albert Namatjira. The diversity of material is evidence both of the interest taken in him by persons in many different walks of life and of the various ways in which the passer-by saw him.

Not all the statements made about him, particularly in recent years, were worthy of equal respect. The journalist seeking a story, or the visitor who sought out a celebrity, did not see or know all that was seen and known by those associated more closely with the artist. Contemporary stories about particular incidents were not all true in detail.

Yet, with patience and skill the author has brought together all the available evidence, and, as a result, this book gives a picture of the man and a fuller account of the circumstances in which he lived than has been given before.

The picture of Albert Namatjira that emerges from the shadows is a picture of an exceptional man. Albert was not only a man of unusual talent. He was a man of unusual character. I differ from some of those who have discussed his life in that I do not see him or his difficulties as 'typical' of his race. There were some exceptional elements both in the man himself and in the situations to which he was exposed that make his story unlike that of other Aborigines. Those who did him ill were different from those who have done ill to others of his race. Anyone who moralises on Albert's life and the life of other Aborigines should be careful about identifying his personal story with the story of the Aborigines in their transition from one way of life to another, for the injury done to him was, in many ways, personal and peculiar.

A great part of Albert's difficulties arose because of separation from his own people and the strain he felt was largely a strain between him and his own people. The confusion he felt came from the pull on him of his own origin and not because of rejection by the white community towards which he was moving. Indeed, the more honour he found among white admirers and the further he went into the white community, the greater became the conflict within himself and the greater the difficulty for him as a member of Aboriginal society. How little most of us can know about that conflict and strain.

With sympathy and care, the author has written a book that helps us to know the story more clearly even although parts of the story are still hidden.

It was my privilege some time ago to unveil a stone memorial to Albert Namatjira at Hermannsburg. It is an equal privilege to have a small part in commending this written memorial to the notice of all Australians.

PREFACE

ALBERT NAMATJIRA was the first Australian aborigine to achieve recognition as an artist. His painting projected him into the white man's world, but from the climax of his success and public acclaim until the last tragic year of his life, this nomad of a Stone Age race was a *wanderer between two worlds,* confused by the anomalies of civilization.

Because the publicity about Namatjira created an unbalanced view of the man himself, an anonymous South Australian wrote asking me to 'produce an honest and faithful account of a native Australian who left to the world a legacy of the finest interpretation of the beauty of his tribal country in Central Australia'. This I have tried to do.

Seacliff,
South Australia.   JOYCE D. BATTY.

ACKNOWLEDGEMENTS

The author gratefully acknowledges the assistance of the following: The *Advertiser* and the *News* and *Sunday Mail* (Adelaide); the Adelaide Public Library and Reading Room Research Service; the South Australian Parliamentary Library; the New Zealand *Herald;* the Melbourne *Sun* and Melbourne *Herald;* the *Sydney Morning Herald; Australasian Post;* the Honorable Paul Hasluck, Minister for Territories; the Honorable J. N. Nelson, M.H.R., Northern Territory; the Honorable J. F. S. Wise; Mr. W. Mackinnon (formerly Senior Inspector and Officer in Charge of the Southern Division of the Northern Territory Police); Mr. V. D. Seymour, Superintendent Gaoler at Alice Springs; Mr. M. Doherty, former Principal Registrar of the High Court of Australia; Professor A. P. Elkin, Emeritus Professor of Anthropology, University of Sydney; Mr. T. G. H. Strehlow, M.A., Reader in Australian Linguistics, University of Adelaide; Mr. Douglas Lockwood, Mr. P. J. Rice, Pastor F. W. Albrecht and the late Pastor S. O. Gross; Mr. and Mrs. E. Fietz; Mr. Claude Hotchin, O.B.E., Perth, W.A.; Mr. Bert Doering, Secretary, Finke River Mission; Pastor and Mrs. Philip Scherer and Mrs. J. E. Lemaire; Messrs. J. Pearson, Garth Mitchell and David Fietz; Peter Bladen; Judith Kirk, Norma Malempre, Joy Hallam and David Ackland for their generous assistance with typing of manuscript; and Mr. Reg Campbell. The author also expresses her appreciation to the many people who provided personal impressions of Namatjira and much material which would otherwise have been difficult to obtain. Especial appreciation is due for invaluable co-operation by the Ansett-A.N.A. Airline.

Finally, the author's thanks are due to her friends and family for their encouragement and patience during the time devoted to completing the book.

ILLUSTRATIONS

between pp. 96 and 97

15

NAMATJIRA
Wanderer Between Two Worlds

1

UNDER the date, 28 July 1902, the Superintendent of the Lutheran Mission at Hermannsburg, in Central Australia, entered in the Mission records the birth of a first son to two primitive aborigines, Namatjira and Ljukuta. The baby was nameless and would, in the normal course of events, have remained so until he was old enough to appreciate the significance of the tribal name that would be bestowed on him.

Namatjira and Ljukuta were members of the Aranda tribe. For countless centuries before the coming of the white man, the aborigines had been born, had lived and had died within an unchanging pattern of law and custom. Each tribe had its own mythology and a strangely complex social order that was passed on from generation to generation by the old men.

One of the Aranda traditions was that a name should not be bestowed until a child was initiated into the complex social structure of the tribe during rites whose origins were lost in far-distant time. The son of Namatjira and Ljukuta would have been named at about the age of fourteen. But on Christmas Eve, 1905, after three years of religious instruction, his parents were baptised in the little church at Hermannsburg. Namatjira and Ljukuta became Jonathan and Emelia. At the same time, their tribal union was given Christian blessing and their son baptised and given the name Albert—simply Albert, because at Hermannsburg Mission, aborigines were given only one name.

Albert became Albert Namatjira only after he had won some recognition as an artist. When he was about to hold his first exhibition in 1938 it was deemed necessary for him to have a surname, presumably on the assumption that a Christian name was scarcely sufficient to sign a painting. After all, one could not imagine Sir Joshua Reynolds signing his paintings Joshua! So it was then that Albert adopted his father's name as a surname. He always remained Albert to everyone in the Alice Springs area but to the outside world he was Namatjira, and the name had a romantic aura that prosaic Albert could never hope to achieve.

Hermannsburg, where Albert was to spend all his younger life, is almost in the heart of the continent. It is set on the banks of the Finke River in a red land with spinifex and stunted trees, bordered by the Macdonnell, Krichauff and Gosse Ranges, whose forbidding purple escarpments are gashed with great ravines.

The nearest white settlement in those days was Stuart, named after the explorer, John MacDouall Stuart. Stuart had been mapped and gazetted in 1888 when the South Australian Government was fixing sites for railheads for a proposed railway across the centre of the continent. It was only two miles from Alice Springs, the repeater station on the Overland Telegraph that linked Darwin in the north with Adelaide in the south. The Alice Springs station had been opened in 1872, its site having been determined by a water-hole named Alice Springs in honour of his wife by Mr. (later Sir) Charles Todd, the Superintendent of Telegraphs. When the railway was eventually extended to Stuart, a certain amount of confusion arose. Telegrams went to Alice Springs, trains to Stuart. Some people called the place Stuart, some Alice Springs. An additional difficulty arose from the fact that, in addition to Stuart, stops on the Central Australian railway included Stewart's Range, Sturt and Stuart's Creek; so, about 1930, the name of the railway station was changed to Alice Springs and very few people nowadays are aware that the town's real name is Stuart.

Today, Hermannsburg, a self-contained village of white buildings with a modern school and hospital surrounding a simple stone church, is no longer remote. It has its own airstrip, is only about three hours' drive from Alice Springs and has its inevitable shortwave radio link with the outside world. But in the days when young Albert attended the school for aborigines conducted by the Superintendent of the Mission, the Rev. Carl Strehlow, Hermannsburg was remote indeed. If it comes to that, so was Stuart itself, with its population of less than a score of white people.

The Hermannsburg Lutheran Mission had been established not only to take Christianity to the aborigines but also to educate them. Teaching the native children the rudiments of reading, writing and arithmetic brought its own special problems. Apart from the fact that the aboriginal children had never known any sort of discipline, they had no written language to provide a starting point. The Rev. Strehlow had to learn the Aranda language before he could begin teaching them the white man's faith and the white man's ways. In the early days of the Mission, the pupils were difficult and irresponsible and strained Christian patience to its limits.

Albert was the exception. His aptitude for learning made him stand out among his fellows. He never rebelled against discipline and was even eager to please. If he had been a white child he might even have been called a prig; but it was not priggishness that made Albert so tractable. It was as though he was already aware of meanings to existence beyond the beliefs of his people.

Although he had been baptised into the Christian faith, however, the countless generations of tribal living inherited in his blood could not be denied. When he was thirteen Albert disappeared and was not seen again for six months. He had been taken by the old men of the Aranda tribe to distant ceremonial grounds for initiation into manhood.

When he returned to the Mission, Albert was regarded by his people as a child no longer. He was a man with a man's responsibility to the unwritten but nevertheless strict and timeless laws of the tribe. Tribal standing apart, Albert did mature quickly. He began to show an interest in the trades being taught the older natives—carpentry, saddlery, building, and so on.

In those early days of his manhood, Albert's skilful hands seemed to be able to master any trade and, for a while, he worked diligently enough at several. But soon he began spending much time with another tribe in the neighbourhood of the Mission. Then, when he was eighteen, he again disappeared. This time it was fairly obvious what had happened. The reason for his frequent absences from the Mission had been Ilkalita, a daughter of Wapiti, the Kukatja ceremonial chief of Merini; but she had been denied him. Firstly, she belonged to a tribal kinship group that, under the complexities of tribal law, was forbidden to him. Secondly, she was not a baptised Christian. So, to avoid both tribal and Mission strictures, Albert eloped with his Ilkalita to neutral country beyond the Aranda and Mission boundaries.

The young people lived on cattle stations until, three years later some wandering Arandas told them that they had been forgiven for eloping. Then they returned to Hermannsburg—with their three young children.

At the Mission they were received by the acting Superintendent, Mr. A. H. Heinrich, the schoolmaster. Mr. Strehlow had died in October, 1922.

Having resumed the Mission's way of life, Albert could no longer live the old communal tribal life; and living the white man's way requires money. But jobs were scarce just then because a widespread drought was ravaging the cattle industry and station owners were faced with financial difficulties. Albert persuaded an Afghan camel driver to give him a job. In those days camels were the only means of carrying freight between the railhead at Oodnadatta and Stuart and Hermannsburg.

Albert covered the 300 miles to Oodnadatta and back

many times. He acquired such a thorough knowledge of the inhospitable country that lay between these centres that he was the obvious person to take a horse-drawn express buggy from the Mission to the railhead to pick up Mr. Heinrich and the girl he had married while on leave in Adelaide. This was in February, 1923. Mrs. Heinrich had never seen a full-blood aborigine and was somewhat apprehensive when she found that, for the remainder of their thousand-mile journey from the city to her remote new home, she and her husband would be in the hands of a young native. But she soon realized that Albert was not only dependable but also that his one concern was his passengers' comfort. Each night he made sure that the camping site was protected from the chill winds of the desert night, lit a big fire, prepared the evening meal and unpacked the sleeping gear before retiring to another campfire that he made for himself at a little distance.

By the end of the arduous four-week journey, Mrs. Heinrich had come to regard Albert as a friend—and their friendship endured over the years.

In spite of his deep respect for tribal tradition, Albert was also aware of his obligations as a member of the Lutheran Church and wanted Ilkalita to become a Christian too. After four months of instruction from a visiting Pastor, the Rev. J. Reidel, Ilkalita was baptised in November, 1923, and given the name Rubina. As was the case with his parents, the union by consent of Albert and Rubina was formally blessed and their children baptised as Enos, Oscar and Maisie.

The drought continued. Season after season passed and brought no relief. It not only destroyed countless hundreds of cattle but human life, too, was threatened as health wilted. Albert did what he could for the people and the animals at the Mission, but even his aboriginal instinct for coping with harsh conditions was powerless against the enemy—the scorching sun that robbed the land of all its surface waters and withered the vegetation. Even the kangaroos, the toughest and most tenacious of all Australia's animals, died

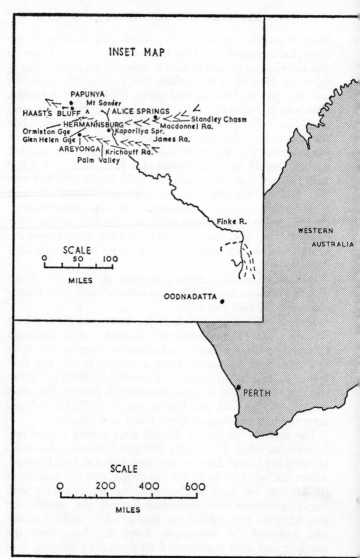

INSET MAP

PAPUNYA
• Mt Sonder
HAAST'S BLUFF ▲   Y ALICE SPRINGS
HERMANNSBURG ◄   Standley Chasm
Ormiston Gge •   • Macdonnel Ra.
Glen Helen Gge | ◉ Kaporilya Spr.
AREYONGA   Krichauff Ra.   James Ra.
Palm Valley

Finke R.

WESTERN
AUSTRALIA

SCALE
0   50   100
MILES

OODNADATTA

PERTH

SCALE
0   200   400   600
MILES

Australia with inset map sh

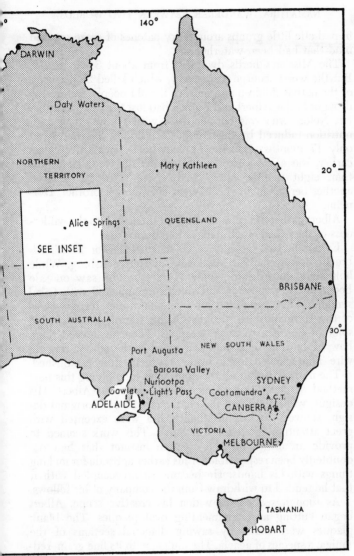

Alice Springs and environs

in pathetic little groups around dry patches of craze-cracked mud that had been waterholes.

The Mission's herds dwindled from about 3,000 to 280. But the worst scourge was scurvy, which killed 25 per cent of the native children and most of the old people. Before the drought broke, Albert and Rubina had lost their baby daughter, Nelda, who was born in 1928 with symptoms of malnutrition induced by the drought conditions. She had lived only 17 months. Hazel, who had been born three years earlier, was also a sickly child, but she survived. Then, less than eight months after Nelda's death, Albert suffered another bereavement—his 21-year-old younger brother, Hermann.

Albert gathered his family and led them up into the wilderness of the Macdonnell Ranges to mourn.

Earlier in the drought years—in 1926—Pastor F. W. Albrecht was appointed Missionary at Hermannsburg. While holidaying in Adelaide some years later, he saw on sale boomerangs, woomeras and shields ornamented with tribal symbols. They suggested an economic outlet for the skills of the Hermannsburg people. On his return, he persuaded some of the men to carve weapons. Then he showed them how to burn designs into the wood with red-hot fencing wire. Thus a new native industry was successfully established.

The most skilful of all the aborigines in applying this new method of decorating to an ancient craft was Albert. His designs, while retaining the characteristics of aboriginal design, showed marked originality and were executed with great attention to detail and finish. This work seemed to provide an outlet for the creative instinct that had undoubtedly been responsible for his earlier aptitude for making things with his hands. He became so preoccupied with it that he tended to withdraw from the company of his fellows.

As though seeking to widen his creative scope, Albert began cutting and ornamenting oval plaques. The blank plaques were made by sawing diagonal sections of the mulga, a species of acacia. The mulga, with its fine grain, reddish brown heartwood and pale amber halo of sapwood, permitted fine carving which could be polished into a rich patina.

Albert's mulga plaques were decorated with designs of native flowers or Central Australian landscapes with emus and kangaroos, accurately observed, in the foreground. They were evidence of his rapidly developing skill in capturing in graphic form the world—the only world—that he knew. Despite his limited schooling, he began inscribing the plaques with Biblical texts.

In 1932 some of Albert's plaques were seen during a patrol visit by Constable W. Mackinnon (later to become Inspector and Senior Officer-in-Charge of the Southern Division of the Northern Territory Police). Mackinnon ordered a dozen of them. Albert was somewhat surprised to find himself having work commissioned—and especially surprised to learn that he would be paid a handsome 5/- each for the plaques. Up till then the Mission had bought each completed weapon or plaque as he brought it in. Perhaps it was Mackinnon's 'commission' that started Albert thinking about the value of his work, leading him to a realisation of the fact that art is not a commodity to be sold by the yard or the pound but something whose value depended on its degree of desirability to a potential customer.

Mackinnon was delighted with the plaques Albert made for him. They depicted Mackinnon's patrol in the desert, with the constable on the first camel, followed by a spare mount, two pack camels, another spare mount, and his 'black tracker' bringing up the rear on a sixth camel. The sparse trees and clumps of spinifex in the background captured faithfully the aspect of the country. Each plaque was inscribed: 'Greetings from the South-west Patrol'.

But pleased though he was with his plaques, Mackinnon did not realise that Albert's talent would eventually launch him into fame and fortune—and into a pathetic no-man's land between two cultures! In those days no one regarded Albert as anything more than an aborigine who happened

27

to be clever with his hands, even though his intelligence and integrity did make him stand out among the Hermannsburg people.

Albert made many white friends; but none of them really ever came to know and understand the mind that lay beyond the dark eyes. He was an enigma, introspective, uncommunicative. Even though he had adopted the white man's religion and had learned many of the white man's trade skills, what had been bred in the blood for thousands of years could not easily be eradicated by brief contact with the Christian faith. He would often leave the Mission and, according to his primitive, in-born instinct, would go walkabout with his family and tribe.

But although he had been initiated into the tribal mysteries and was honour-bound to the laws of his ancestors, he never allowed himself to be drawn into the secret and sacred ceremonies that were still kept alive by some of the older Aranda men. However, he did remain conscious of the basic principle on which all aboriginal law and social structure was built—the principle of sharing. It was the primitive communistic principle of share-and-share-alike that had enabled the aborigines to survive for aeons in one of the world's harshest environments. Throughout his life, Albert continued to honour his tribal obligation of sharing all he received with his many relations. It gave him great satisfaction to give presents—and not only to his own people.

When the time came for the Heinrichs to leave Hermannsburg, Albert made a special plaque for them out of gratitude for their friendship. In the nine years since he had driven them up from the Oodnadatta railhead, a deep affection had grown up between him and the schoolmaster and his wife. As the Mission truck that was to take them to Alice Springs was loaded with their possessions, the aborigines gathered to bid them farewell. The last to pay his parting respects was Albert. He handed Heinrich the mulga plaque carved specially for the occasion. It bore the legend: 'Sweeten the cup of life whenever you can.'

Over the years, the isolation of Hermannsburg was broken down by the extension of the railhead from Oodnadatta to Alice Springs and by the rapid growth in numbers of motor vehicles of all sorts. As a result, people from the south visited the Mission much more frequently. In June, 1932, a party of tourists from Victoria who had been exploring the Macdonnells camped at the Mission overnight. In the party was Miss Una Teague, who was so enchanted with the strange, rugged beauty of Central Australia that she returned the following year with her artist sister, Violet.

Violet, too, was excited by this virtually unknown land whose shapes and colours were like nothing she had ever seen. She set about capturing it on canvas. But at Hermannsburg the Teagues were reminded that beauty and cruelty are not by any means incompatible. They were horrified to hear of the Mission's sufferings during the great drought. They learned, moreover, that the tragedy could be repeated because the Mission had no permanent water supply—and a permanent water supply was its only safeguard. It was not impracticable to take water to Hermannsburg. The only barrier was poverty.

When they returned to Melbourne the Teague sisters launched a campaign to raise funds for the Mission. A canvass of her artist friends by Violet resulted in their giving well over a hundred of their paintings for a charity art exhibition. To these she added many of her own paintings of Central Australia. Authors contributed autographed copies of their books for sale, and the daily newspaper, *The Argus*, opened a subscription fund. The result was over £2,000 for a water scheme at Hermannsburg.

A start was made at once with the laying of a pipeline from Kaporilja Springs to the Mission. Its construction provided a break from the routine day-to-day life of the Mission. The aborigines gathered to watch—and even Albert put aside his work to join his tribesmen. But he was not merely curious; his observant senses were at work.

Some little time later, Albert showed Pastor Albrecht a

mulga boomerang which he had decorated with a wire-burnt design that showed men laying pipes in a trench. Albrecht recognised in this work a considerable advance of skill. It was plain that Albert's desire was to capture as faithfully as was in his power the country to which he belonged. It was therefore not surprising that he showed keen interest in the visit of two artists, Rex Battarbee and John A. Gardner during the winter of 1934. Albert studied a display of their paintings at length. Here was the key to a whole new world of creation or re-creation for him. He asked Albrecht how much the artists would get for such paintings and was told about 15 guineas each. Albert pondered this and then asserted that he could also paint like that.

Albrecht was doubtful, but Albert was so insistent that Albrecht talked about the ambitious aboriginal with Battarbee. Battarbee saw some of Albert's work and advised that painting materials should be bought for him.

When Albert got his first box of water-colours, he was as eager as any small boy with his first paint box. But painting with water colours was not nearly as simple as Albert had anticipated. Colours would run into one another and he could not get exactly the colours he wanted. Then he would get the paper too wet and the paint would smudge. Albert persevered and got some measure of control over his materials but it was obvious to Albrecht that, compared with his mulga designing, his watercolour efforts were crude. Albrecht advised him to put the paints aside until Batterbee returned and could show him the basic techniques of the art. But Albert was too impatient to wait. He splashed his colours on sheet after sheet of paper until it had all been used. Then he started on the reverse sides.

Albert had been experimenting with his watercolours for about a year when, in May, 1935, Mr. F. C. G. Wallent, of the Lutheran Mission Board, visited Hermannsburg. Wallent's interest in his work so pleased Albert that he made him a gift of one of his paintings—or, more precisely, two paintings, because there was one on each side the paper. One was obviously an early effort, with little detail and feeble colouring but the landscape on the reverse side was sharply delineated and showed considerable sense of perspective. The dominant feature was a kangaroo in flight, its movement frozen in flowing lines. Wallent kept the painting and handed it on to his son, Oswald, in whose possession it is now. In 1949, after Albert's talent had been recognised, he was shown those paintings and acknowledged them. On one he wrote 'My first painting' and on the other 'The fleeing kangaroo'. He also wrote the date of their execution, 1935, and signed them.

Albert's family continued to grow. He now had six children to support. Enos, Oscar, Maisie and Hazel were all of school age. Then there were Ewald, born in 1930, and Martha, born in 1932. His last child, Violet, was born in 1935 but only lived five months. Albert was always anxious to earn as much as he could for their sake. Most of the aborigines were content with the Mission rations and the few pounds they earned working at some trade or other; but Albert had learned ambition from the white man. He wanted to paint and earn big money like the white artists. He made some money from his mulga souvenirs and augmented his income by working as a ringer or station hand on neighbouring cattle stations. But he lived only for Battarbee's return.

Battarbee's third visit to Hermannsburg was made in the winter of 1936. He took Albert as a companion and together the two men set out on camels for Palm Valley, a canyon in the Krichauff Ranges, where, in the ancient bed of what was once a river, is an oasis of palms, survivals from a distant geological period. The species which has been named *Livistonia mariae* is found nowhere else in the world. In vivid contrast to their rich green are towering outcrops of red sandstone, weathered through the ages into fantastic forms. In Palm Valley there was rich material for the artists but, for Albert, the valley meant more than scenes to paint; for here were ceremonial sites sacred to the Arandas.

Battarbee and Albert established their camp in the valley

and artist and pupil worked together. At first Battarbee had
Albert working with coloured crayons on cardboard to
familiarise him with the use of colour. But Albert was impatient to paint in watercolour, so Battarbee gave in to him.
For a fortnight he helped Albert, showing him how to mix
colours, how to wash the colours on, how to use his brushes.
In a very short space of time Albert was producing work that
astonished his tutor. He could reproduce a scene before
him with great fidelity. But he had yet to learn the principles
of composition.

For six weeks Albert guided Battarbee through the ranges
he knew so well from tribal associations and at the same
time Battarbee guided Albert towards an understanding of
the white man's art he aspired to. When Pastor Albrecht
saw the work Albert had accomplished on the expedition he
realised where Albert's future lay. It was his duty now to
help Albert to develop to the utmost his undoubted talents.

2

IN March, 1937, Pastor Albrecht went south to attend the Lutheran Synodical Conference at Nuriootpa, in South Australia. He took with him ten of Albert's watercolours which he displayed in an exhibition of handicrafts by natives of the Mission. The paintings were priced at five and ten shillings each, but although they aroused considerable interest, only four were sold. To lessen Albert's disappointment, Pastor Albrecht bought another two himself.

When he returned, the Pastor found Albert anxious to know how his work had been received. The fact that six had been sold was encouraging and Albert worked on his watercolours more assiduously than ever. When Rex Battarbee next came to the Mission, he found his pupil producing work that was something more than promising. He took the best three with him to Adelaide and showed them at an exhibition of his own work.

Although they were for display only, a collection box yielded eight pounds. Art critics, normally cautious in their comments about the work of any new artist, were unrestrained in their appreciation of the paintings of the semi-primitive Aranda who signed his works, Albert.

Louis McCubbin, Director of the South Australian National Art Gallery, wrote: 'It is remarkable how this aborigine has grasped so readily the European conception of art. His painting of Mount Hermannsburg is outstanding in its realism, light and form and solidity of hills. Altogether, the aborigine's knowledge of tone and colour value is extra-ordinary.'

Hans (later Sir Hans) Heysen, one of Australia's best known artists, took the keenest interest in Albert's paintings. Battarbee, gratified by the reception accorded his pupil, asserted that no white man could have achieved so much in the same time. He added that he was planning a full exhibition of Albert's paintings in Melbourne and that Albert might attend. Later, however, Battarbee had second thoughts about the advisability of such a visit, for Albert had never been farther than Alice Springs and Oodnadatta, and the city might be a disturbing influence on his artist's vision, a vision that had been nurtured by the isolated vastness of his tribal country untouched by the white man's zeal for progress.

Battarbee's feelings in the matter were supported by the Victorian artist, William Rowell, who said, after a visit to Central Australia: 'I spent some time with that remarkable aborigine, Albert of Hermannsburg. His work is painstakingly accurate, thoughtful and with a good grasp of the medium. He has an amazing flair for colour and design which if left alone might produce some wonderful results. It will be a great pity if Albert is ever allowed to visit the cities. Every means should be taken to see that he does not.' Rowell predicted—accurately—'The white man may gain by the adoption of civilised art by a primitive aborigine, but eventually he will be judged by our standards and outlook, which may place him at a disadvantage.'

At the time Albert's work was known only to the few with an interest in his art, although efforts were being made to bring his paintings to the notice of the general public.

One such effort (in August, 1938) was an exhibition in the Lower Town Hall in Melbourne of native handicrafts, including watercolours by Albert. It attracted such interest that, on several occasions, police had to be summoned to control the crowds, and to protect the exhibits. One of the policemen on guard duty was among the fortunate few to acquire one of Albert's signed paintings. It cost him twenty-five shillings.

The reception accorded his work gave Albert still further incentive to work towards his goal of becoming a professional artist. It was then two years since he had learned something of the techniques of watercolour painting and he was eager to make money with his brushes. There was now yet another child to support. Keith had been born on the 13th June, which meant that Albert, Rubina and seven children had to cram into his tiny hut. Albert told Pastor Albrecht he wanted to build a new house of stone and timber. The Pastor was sympathetic, but pointed out that such a house would be costly and advised Albert to wait until his paintings began to sell.

So Albert waited anxiously for the exhibition Battarbee was arranging in Melbourne. His impatience was temporarily abated by a visit to Hermannsburg of the wife of the Governor of Victoria, Lady Huntingfield, who was surprised to find that many of the 300 natives at the Mission were engaged in crafts of some sort. She saw women making kangaroo skin rugs from pelts tanned by the men; stockmen who were superb horsemen, carpenters and saddlers. But inevitably, it was Albert's watercolours that claimed her closest attention. Lady Huntingfield met Albert and talked with him at length. He had won still another supporter.

Three months later, on 5 December, Lady Huntingfield opened Albert's first exhibition in the Fine Arts Galleries in Melbourne and, in the course of her speech, told how she had visited Hermannsburg and seen for herself the natural creative talents of the aborigines. She had been amazed to find artistic aptitude even among the children. They learned to write and draw more quickly than white children. 'We must realise,' she said, 'that these people are worthy of recognition when they respond in such a wonderful way to tuition and sympathy.'

The paintings in this exhibition were the first to bear the signature, Albert Namatjira. They were the result of a 400-

mile journey into country that would delight any artist, according to Rex Battarbee who had accompanied his pupil, and they had an immediate appeal. Within minutes of Lady Huntingfield's closing words, red 'sold' stickers began to appear on the frames. Within three days all 41 paintings were sold—an unprecedented success for a complete newcomer in the city's galleries.

The Age stated that the exhibition had no parallel: 'It may be out of place to review this exhibition from the usual critical standpoint; yet there are qualities in the work of the "native" artist which command respect. He is clearly a careful and intelligent observer of the scene he sets out to portray and where one might expect a primitive reversion to a flat surface, the sense of space and light is, in most cases, well in evidence.'

Mr. R. H. Croll, who had written the introduction to the catalogue, referred to the natural artistic sense of the native Australians who had been practising their art for thousands of years on the walls of caves and rock shelters, and on their weapons and totemic objects. It was the aboriginal custom to decorate the most ordinary articles—shields, spear throwers and boomerangs—with bold designs, often vividly coloured with red and yellow ochre, white clay and black charcoal. Even the women's dilly bags were woven with definite designs, and the sacred tribal churingas and bullroarers often bore intricate designs of unique artistry. So Albert Namatjira was a natural artist by virtue of inheritance. He advanced to civilised art with no other teacher than his own keen senses.

'I am assured,' Croll wrote, 'the paintings in Albert Namatjira's first exhibition are his own unaided work. A competent critic has declared that the most remarkable feature is the invariably fine selection of subject. The clarity of the sunlight in the arid Centre is excellently conveyed and the strange and startling hues of those remarkable ranges, the Macdonnells, have been faithfully observed and just as faithfully portrayed.'

But the critics were not unanimous in their appreciation of Albert Namatjira's painting. Some suggested that it had only curiosity value. Harold Herbert wrote: 'Although Albert Namatjira is the first aboriginal to exhibit paintings in a truly realistic manner, there is no need for a fanfare of trumpets. I do not accept his paintings as outstanding art.'

The mixture of extravagant praise and disparagement accompanying the complete sell-out of this first exhibition was to become the pattern with all his future shows.

Albert's paintings were at last earning money for him.

'That's good,' he said. 'Now I paint more pictures, earn more money. Buy nice things for everybody. Build myself a nice house.'

Then he set off with his family on a long walkabout to his favourite painting grounds.

On 2 November 1939, Albert's second exhibition was opened in Adelaide by Doctor Charles Duguid. A large crowd gathered in the Royal Art Society's Gallery and once again the conclusion of the opening speech was the signal for a rush to buy. Within half an hour, 20 of the 41 exhibits had been sold at prices ranging from 2½ to 7 guineas. There was some competition for two head studies of aborigines and several other exhibits were claimed by two or three intending purchasers. The Adelaide National Gallery made history by being the first Australian gallery to purchase a watercolour by an aborigine. The painting chosen was a landscape of Haasts Bluff entitled 'Illum-Baura'. It was considered the best in the collection, with its opalescent blues and greens merging at the base of the Bluff to suggest the peculiar translucence that characterises the Central Australian ranges.

The Adelaide critics were kinder than the Melbourne critics. All predicted a great future for Namatjira.

Inevitably the public was interested in the exhibition, if only for the fact that Namatjira was an aborigine. The gallery was crowded each day. The extraordinary demand for Albert's work prompted an urgent message to Hermannsburg to send more paintings to the city at the earliest opportunity.

Albert's debut in the art world was a unique success. Initial exhibitions in two capital cities in the space of a year was a record. It seemed certain that future exhibitions would be equally successful. Then war broke on the world and cultural events were severely curtailed. But, encouraged by success, Albert continued to paint. The war meant little in Hermannsburg, a thousand miles from the nearest city.

In 1940, evidence of enemy activity within Australia resulted in all persons and organisations with German connections being subjected to security investigation. The Hermannsburg Mission, being of German origin, was automatically included. Although the Mission was above suspicion, a liaison officer was appointed to Hermannsburg as a formal security measure. The officer was the Mission's old friend Rex Battarbee, an ex-Serviceman of the First World War.

The visit of security officials to the Mission did not affect Albert Namatjira. It is doubtful whether he had any real comprehension of the reason why his former tutor should come to live there. The war was too far away to have any reality beyond the fact that two of his sons, Enos and Oscar, had gone to Alice Springs to 'work alonga Army with white feller soldier, get five bob a week and tucker.' But the coming of Australian and American soldiers to Central Australia did mean something to Albert. Many who came to Hermannsburg during defence exercises were intrigued to find a native painting watercolours just like a white artist's. They bought them as souvenirs and soon Albert was overwhelmed with orders.

The soaring sales of the paintings, which sold at from one to five guineas, could easily have got out of hand, so an advisory council was formed not only to supervise sales, but also to ensure that Albert did not abandon his standards in the interests of a big turnover. Battarbee was chairman of the council, with Miss Hilda Wurst (headmistress of the

Mission school), Pastor S. O. Gross (newly appointed Assistant Superintendent), and Mr. A. P. Latz, of the Mission staff, as advisers.

Albert was grateful to the council for its guidance. On its advice, he restricted himself to an average of about 50 watercolours a year and prices were fixed at from three to fifteen guineas. The wartime shortage of materials, however, threatened to curtail Albert's output even further. Good quality watercolour paper became almost unobtainable. But Albert's native ingenuity overcame the difficulty. He made 'canvases' from the timber of beanwood trees by cutting sections measuring 10 by 16 inches and sandpapering them to a satin-smooth finish. The new medium, devised from necessity, was, however, no second-rate substitute. It was to be the basis of some of his most successful works. Pastor Gross bought one that captured the cool waters of a waterhole on the upper Finke River cradled in a small canyon of warm red sandstone cliffs. Beyond a harmony of tall river gums, a purple mountain reared in silhouette against a faintly clouded sky. Albert painted about 50 pictures on beanwood, but Pastor Gross was satisfied that his was the finest.

While Albert was painting on beanwood, he often went to Palm Valley, sometimes accompanied by the three young Pareroultja brothers. One day a party of soldiers on reconnaissance exercises came upon Albert and the Pareroultjas all busy painting. One of them, Private Andrew Schubert, had met Albert at a church service. Albert quietly acknowledged his greeting but in a moment was back in the world of his painting.

'I had seen some of Albert's paintings which my friends had bought, including scenes of Palm Valley,' Schubert reported, 'but really only understood what a fine artist Albert was when I saw the valley for the first time. I looked at his painting and it was a faithful reproduction of the scene in front of him. Towering walls of weathered sandstone, varying in colour from deep vermilion to shaded ochre rose sheer from the ancient river bed. Softly fronded palm trees were reflected in the crystal clear waters of rock pools, a solitary ghost gum's pure white trunk a striking contrast to the massive red boulders. I watched as Albert put the finishing touches to his painting with sure, deft strokes of his brush. He was a born artist and, as his interpretation of the scene before him proved, a great artist.'

The demand for Albert's paintings as souvenirs of Central Australia became so great that his advisory council had difficulty in retaining a sufficient number for an exhibition. However, by April, 1944, the council had put by 40, which were sent to Melbourne for exhibition in the Mural Hall of the Myer Emporium. This, Namatjira's second Melbourne exhibition, was opened on 17 April 1944, by Mr. A. W. Coles, M.P., who said that a large majority of white people thought aborigines were without intelligence. But they would change their minds when they saw the paintings by Namatjira who had had only two months' art instruction. He hoped that, after the war, the aborigines would get a better deal and be accepted as citizens instead of being brushed aside as in the past.

The second Melbourne exhibition was also a complete success. All 38 paintings were sold, prices ranging from 10 to 35 guineas, a significant advance on the one to five guineas of the first exhibition.

Doctor Charles Duguid, of Adelaide, who already owned seven Namatjira paintings, bought one work which, according to Battarbee, could take its place in an exhibition of watercolours anywhere in the world.

Mr. Nelson T. Johnson, American Minister to Australia, who was greatly interested in the social status of Australian natives, visited the exhibition and bought a painting. This impressed him so much he decided to visit Hermannsburg to see for himself how the aboriginal artist lived.

'One ought not to know anything about Namatjira, but judge his pictures solely on their merits,' wrote *The Age* critic. 'But this asks too much of one who, though a critic, is also human. One comes to such an exhibition with a measure, however small, of anthropology in his mind, and in a mood to make artistic allowances; but for this precaution there is no need. Albert Namatjira stands on his own two artistic feet.'

Namatjira was becoming something of a national figure. Leading newspapers ran feature articles on him and soldiers who had met him were no doubt pleased to read in the Army magazine, *Salt*, the headlines: 'Aboriginal paints his world. Namatjira Wins Fame in 3 One-man Shows.'

'Another jolt to the complacent illusion that the aboriginal has nothing to teach the white Australians is the Melbourne exhibition of the work of Albert Namatjira, gifted citizen of Central Australia,' this article ran. 'His work should help remind us that in the midst of all the attention being given to native cultures in other parts of the world, the Australian "black" has a distinct and worthy claim to notice. Full-blooded, almost untouched by civilisation, still living in his own tribal surroundings, Namatjira is unique. His work is a living answer to those who decry his people as untalented savages. It is easy to see in his work the aboriginals' deep, abiding love of earth.'

Mr. (later Sir) Daryl Lindsay, Director of the Melbourne National Gallery, strongly criticised the aboriginal artist for becoming westernised. He regretted that an aborigine was producing a secondhand version of European art instead of developing his own native art, adding that Namatjira's water-colours had little to commend them except a superficial technical ability and topographical interest and that, with the influence of European pictorial art, the aborigine seemed to have lost something vital.

This brought Battarbee to Namatjira's defence. The aboriginal artist stood on his own merits as an artist, Battarbee retorted. He pointed out that white men could be influenced by any art school in the world, so why shouldn't the black man? When Australian painters adopted French styles, no one criticised them for doing this. Therefore his highbrow critics would be well advised to regard Namatjira as a watercolourist and not an aborigine.

Meanwhile, Albert Namatjira was unaware that controversy over his work was raging in sophisticated Melbourne art circles. He was out on walkabout with Rubina, his three daughters and five sons. And he was, of course, painting. Fifteen hundred miles away from all the disturbing arguments, he was also unaware that he had achieved the unique distinction of being the first aborigine to be listed in *Who's Who in Australia* (1944). In the same year, *The Art of Albert Namatjira*, by South Australian ethnologist, C. P. Mountford, F.R.A.I., was published by the Bread and Cheese Club in Melbourne. It included colour reproductions of some of Albert's paintings. In the concluding chapter, Mountford described his parting from Albert in Palm Valley where he had been collecting legends of the Aranda tribe: 'I wondered what lay ahead of Albert Namatjira. I continue to wonder. Will fame, that fickle mistress, court and then defeat him? Or will he escape to live among his fellows, happy and unspoilt, a living example of the innate artistry of his race.'

3

IN 1945 came the first Sydney exhibition of Namatjira's work. It was opened by Professor A. P. Elkin, Professor of Anthropology in Sydney University. The rush to buy was even more frantic than at earlier exhibitions. Within minutes of Professor Elkin's closing words, the entire collection of 44 paintings was sold. The receipts totalled about £1,000. Among the buyers were American Servicemen. Three works were bought for the Dunedin Art Society of New Zealand, a dozen for England and several for American galleries.

The public enthusiasm for Namatjira's work was not in the least dampened by the Sydney critics, who regarded the aboriginal merely as a good craftsman but an inferior artist. Nevertheless there were some favourable Press comments.

The Sunday Sun and Guardian said: 'Mr. Albert Namatjira has had to submit to some impertinences of criticism à la mode, because he is an aboriginal. But all the bunkum showered upon our Aranda artist need not disturb him. The public which prefers pictorial observation and good technique in its pictures has so far responded by buying Albert Namatjira's paintings. The truth is that Mr. Namatjira's landscapings of Central Australia are convincing because they represent the ranges and plains as the aboriginal as well as the white man sees them and record them with a competence that infuriates the critics today. To sum up, the Aranda artist is a very good artist indeed.'

43

The Sydney exhibition fanned the coals of controversy into renewed heat. Professor Elkin broadcast an answer to the critics who decried Namatjira's departure from the primitive art of his ancestors. He explained the origin and significance of aboriginal art and pointed out that some critics had confused the art of the Arandas with bark paintings. In fact, the Arandas had never produced bark paintings; their art was characterized by concentric circles, parallel lines and conventional patterns inscribed on sacred objects and could not be regarded as painting at all. The only paintings by Central Australian tribes were on the rock faces of caves and depicted the hunt for emus and kangaroos and, sometimes, sacred symbols. Professor Elkin asked Namatjira's critics if they expected him to continue drawing circles. Perhaps what they demanded of a full-blood aborigine was not naturalistic pictures of mountains and valleys but his conception of the great legends of the Dreamtime, the Dreamtime being the distant period when the world was formed. Evidently some critics had looked for a watercolour artist of Wagnerian stature, who painted mighty mythical heroes striding across the land, cleaving the ranges into chasms and rivers with their boomerangs.

Another question raised about this time was why Namatjira never appeared at his exhibitions. His advisers explained their belief that the frantic, bustling crowds and traffic of the cities and the curious, gaping public at the exhibitions would be extremely disturbing to the shy nomad who had spent all his 42 years in the untouched tribal country of his people. Even though he knew all the Mission staff well, he rarely made social contact with them except when he brought his paintings in or came to consult with his advisory council about his finances. Although he could speak English quite well, he was never very communicative. But whenever he happened to be at Hermannsburg he attended church services. He enjoyed them and especially liked joining in the hymns with his pleasant tenor voice.

Albert himself never asked to attend any of his exhibitions.

He seemed quite content to leave his affairs to his advisory council, although he did have a cheque book and was at liberty to spend the money he earned just as he wished. Much of his money went to buy provisions for his family and the large number of tribal relatives with whom, by tribal law, he was obliged to share all he had. Albert was, in any case, generous by nature.

Now a man of substance, Albert was at last able to build the house 'alla same white man' that had long been his dream. The primitive grass and bough shelter had become uncomfortably over-crowded and gave little protection from the heat and dust in the summer. So, with the approval of the Mission, he built a two-roomed cottage a few miles from Hermannsburg, making provision for the addition of extra rooms in the future. The cottage proved yet another example of Albert's skill as a craftsman. He built it of local sandstone, which he cut into bricks. He plastered the walls with cement and white-washed them. His timbered roof was covered with galvanised iron. He employed a white contractor to sink a bore, erect a windmill and lay water pipes to the house. With the building of this house, Albert, of his own initiative, had taken the first step towards the white man's way of life. The nomad of the semi-desert lands felt the pride of ownership; and he did something that, for an aborigine so close to his ancestral ways, was quite remarkable, because the aborigines have never been husbandmen: he planted flower and vege-table gardens.

Albert continued to paint regularly and still took Oscar and Enos with him on many of his expeditions. They, too, were becoming adept at painting. The three Pareroultja brothers often joined the Namatjiras. These young Arandas were pro-ducing very promising work and were soon in the limelight, too, for the six Aranda artists between them had virtually established a unique native school of art.

Early in 1946 came still another exhibition—this time in Adelaide again. It was held in the gallery of the Royal South Australian Society of Arts and was opened by Mr. A. R.

Downer, who later became Minister for Immigration. The pattern was now firmly established; 36 of the 41 paintings shown were sold in less than half an hour. Prices, too, were rising—up to 40 guineas. The Governor of South Australia, Sir Charles Willoughby Norrie, was among the buyers. So, too, was a man who travelled 600 miles from Victoria for that express purpose. Four paintings went to Brisbane, Queensland; one to Honolulu; and one to the National Art Gallery in Perth, Western Australia. A Sydney firm bought one as a gift for the British Minister of Aviation, Lord Winster.

Many of the paintings in this particular exhibition featured the graceful ghost gums of Central Australia, clearly Namatjira's favourite subject. Some critics had hinted that he concentrated on the ghost gums because he could not paint any other variety of tree with any success. But at least two of the paintings in this exhibition refuted this. One—considered by many the best in the collection—was a study of Mount Sonder which featured twin gaunt corkwood trees. The other was a group of grass trees that suggested primitive dancers, with the stiff green spines of the foliage like 'skirts' around slender dark trunks.

As with most people, growing affluence implanted in Albert a desire for things that had previously been outside his means. He had long coveted a motor vehicle so that he could travel in comfort to distant painting grounds. He was now 44 years of age and, being a big man—he weighed about 18 stone—he found travelling by camel increasingly arduous. He had first approached Pastor Gross about buying a motor truck back in 1944 but there had been a war on then and motor vehicles were unobtainable. By 1946, however, the war was over and many Service vehicles were being sold in Alice Springs by Army Disposals. On Albert's behalf, Pastor Gross bought a 30-cwt. Chevrolet truck at a disposal sale. Albert and his three sons learned to drive and the Namatjira family, with a full complement of relations and a large store of provisions, set off on their first modern 'walkabout'.

In this year—1946—Albert's fame had become such that

the Department of the Interior, through the National Film
Board, decided to tell his story in a large-scale documentary
in colour. The film unit's producer was C. P. Mountford, who
knew the aborigines well and had personally recorded much
of their life on film. Lee Robinson was assistant producer
and Axel Poignant cameraman. The team travelled thousands
of miles by camel and on foot as well as by motor vehicle.

The shooting of *Namatjira the Painter* began with scenes
reconstructing the age-old way of life of the Aranda tribe,
their cultures and corroborees. Albert's earliest efforts were
shown in a sequence re-creating his first painting lesson
with Rex Battarbee when pupil and tutor had travelled by
camel to distant painting grounds in the wild grandeur of
the central Australian mountains. Albert himself played in
all these scenes and quickly grasped what the director required of him. No self-consciousness came through the lens,
only his quiet dignity.

All in all, 1946 was quite a year for Albert. In August, His
Royal Highness, the Duke of Gloucester, the then Governor-
General of Australia, accompanied by the Duchess, visited
Standley Chasm, the well-known beauty spot in the Mac-
donnell Ranges, 80 miles south-west of Alice Springs, and
watched Albert at work.

The visit was to be informal, but proved even more informal than planned. The Duchess and Pastor Gross were in
the lead as the party approached the entrance of the chasm.
It was she who first saw Albert painting. The official who
was to make the introductions had somehow drifted to the
rear of the straggling party. Without waiting for the group
to sort itself out for official introduction, the Duchess went
straight up to Albert and introduced herself and, when her
husband joined her, introduced him, too. Albert was unper-
turbed by his Royal audience and continued to apply colour
to paper with his customary confident skill while they talked
with him at some length.

Pastor Gross said later: 'I was in an embarrassing situation,
as it was not my duty to introduce Albert to the Duchess.

47

Realising this, Her Royal Highness excused herself to me and went forward alone to shake hands with Albert. This spontaneous gracious gesture set everyone at ease and the remainder of the time spent at Standley Chasm, including a picnic lunch, had an atmosphere of informality.'

The meeting of Royalty with the famous aborigine in that remote majestic setting was a moving occasion for all who witnessed it, although Albert himself was, as usual, uncommunicative.

'It was all right,' was his only comment.

It is doubtful whether Albert fully realised the significance of the visit. He was, perhaps, vaguely aware that a Governor-General lived in a big house in a place called Canberra where the laws of the white man were made. But Albert was soon to learn the meaning of at least one law that applied to him with an increasing income.

Newspaper reports about an aboriginal artist who was earning as much as £1,000 from a single exhibition of his paintings attracted the interest of the Taxation Department. Investigators came and, in their impersonal way, computed his income over the years. In due course, Albert received an income tax assessment which was, naturally, quite incomprehensible to him. His advisory council tried unsuccessfully to explain what it was all about. Actually, they had considered Albert exempt from taxation since aborigines were, with certain exceptions, not citizens of the Commonwealth and were, therefore, not subject to the laws that applied to white Australians. They took the matter up with the Taxation Department on his behalf.

In March, 1947, Albert began complaining of a persistent pain in his chest. He was admitted to the Alice Springs Hospital for observation. Angina pectoris was diagnosed. After a fortnight's treatment, Albert was discharged with a warning from the doctor that he must reduce his weight. As a man of independent means, Albert had been able to afford the best of white man's food and this was unnatural for an aborigine whose breeding had conditioned his body for survival on a

48

meagre diet. Together with the lack of exercise, it was seriously affecting his health.

Albert's friends at Hermannsburg and his family were worried. They advised him to 'go bush' and eat off the land as his forebears had done for countless ages. So, taking his wife with him, he went on a long walkabout. He hunted and killed kangaroos and goannas and roasted them in the coals of the camp fire. Witchetty grubs and honey ants were, of course, eaten live. Rubina was adept at finding these delicacies. Albert returned to Hermannsburg with his weight down and his health up.

'Bush tucker do me good,' he said. 'Wife eat all white man's food. She be skinny, anyway. It can't harm her.'

The return to the Mission meant a return to the problem of income tax. The Taxation Department had rejected the advisory council's objections and insisted that Albert pay tax on all his earnings. The assessment made no allowance for the enormous expense of providing for Albert's numerous tribal relatives. Albert was bewildered by the Taxation Department's demands, but he was told he had to pay. He did—with a cheque on his own bank account.

The obvious injustice, not so much of the taxation but of the manner of its assessment and demand, was brought to the notice of the Federal Parliament. A lengthy and often heated debate aired anomalies affecting the rights of aborigines. But, in spite of several representations that Albert was an unfortunate victim of circumstances and, therefore, should not be called on to pay taxes, it was ruled that the law must be upheld and the debate closed.

The unique nature of the subject of the debate resulted in wide press coverage and comment. Soon afterwards the simple aborigine, living in a world far removed from the stresses of headlines and contention, was again in the news when the press featured this letter:

The Lady-in-Waiting to the Princess Elizabeth is desired by Her Royal Highness to thank the members of the Aranda tribe for so kindly sending the three water colours painted by Albert Namatjira, Edwin Pareroultja and Otto Pareroultja for the Princess' acceptance. Her Royal Highness much admires these paintings and has been graciously pleased to accept them as a token of good will on the occasion of her 21st birthday, and the Lady-in-Waiting is to convey Her Royal Highness' most sincere thanks for the most loyal thought which prompted the Aranda artists to send these paintings.

When told that his painting and those of his fellow artists had been accepted by the Princess and would be displayed in Buckingham Palace with those of world-famed artists, Albert simply said he was pleased the work of other Aranda artists was also gaining recognition.

Although Albert Namatjira had long been a familiar figure in Alice Springs, the townspeople rarely saw his paintings. Six exhibitions had been held in three capital cities but there had not been a single exhibition in Albert's own 'capital', as it were. So one was arranged in Griffiths House. Once again all paintings were sold—at from 18 to 45 guineas. Later in the same year a second Brisbane exhibition was mounted. Seventeen of the 30 watercolours were sold at a preview. Brisbane critics commented on the amazing popularity of Albert's paintings. This popularity could hardly be a matter of curiosity value alone, when the Brisbane Art Gallery had purchased one of his landscapes. Surely the gallery was concerned only with aesthetic values; this purchase suggested that Albert Namatjira had earned a place among the established artists whose paintings were hung there.

4

IN 1948 Albert had his first taste of dishonest dealing. He sought advice from Pastor Gross about a demand for payment of £42 for a crate of paper which an Alice Springs man claimed he had ordered. Albert had been forced to take delivery of the crate and when he opened it had found inferior paper and not the special paper he used for his paintings. Pastor Gross inspected the paper and advised Albert not to pay.

The missionaries at Hermannsburg had been aware for some time of underhand dealings where the work of the growing body of aboriginal artists was concerned. Tourists visiting the Mission had mentioned a man in Alice Springs who was selling Aranda paintings at exorbitant prices. Also, the Aranda Arts Council, which had been formed to protect the artists' interests, noticed they were spending much time in Alice Springs and bringing fewer paintings to the Council. When Albert was questioned, he was evasive at first, but finally admitted that he, too, was selling paintings to a man in Alice Springs who had promised all the artists that he could get them painting paper cheaply. However the paper proved to be inferior while the price demanded for it was what they would have had to pay for quality watercolour paper.

Some weeks after Albert had been advised to ignore the demand, a letter was received demanding payment of £42.

Further advice was sought and payment was now advised and Albert sent off a cheque. A little later, Pastor Gross received a note from the District Officer for Native Affairs saying that the Crown Solicitor in Darwin had advised that Namatjira could not have been compelled to pay for inferior materials.

Pastor Gross then took the matter up and it was agreed that Albert's cheque should be returned. Weeks went by but the cheque did not arrive. Albert's advisers then sent the crate of paper to the firm in Adelaide that supplied his painting materials. It so happened that this firm had also supplied the poorer quality of paper.

Pastor Gross, on furlough to Adelaide, visited the firm and met the saleswoman who had made out the original order for the crate of paper. She particularly remembered it because it had seemed an unusually large order for cheap drawing paper normally sold for use in schools at only threepence per sheet. Pastor Gross explained why he had returned the crate of paper and was told to get in touch with the Prices Commissioner.

Eventually Albert was reimbursed by the man who had tried to defraud him. He was pleased to get the cheque but he was, at the same time, so indignant that, although he seldom wrote letters, he wrote to the acting Director of Native Affairs in Alice Springs requesting that the man who had caused him this trouble should be removed from Central Australia to 'the country he came from, as he is a bad man and we don't want him here.'

The man in question, however, continued to live in Alice Springs and while Albert had no further dealings with him, the younger artists did. Reports continued to reach Hermannsburg that they were selling their paintings cheaply. When questioned, they admitted that a man living in a tent in the town had asked them to paint landscapes for him, and sometimes asked that they leave them unsigned.

About this time a measles epidemic broke out in Alice Springs and some of the artists who were in town were prevented from returning to the Mission. Being short of money, they were easy victims of exploitation.

Then one day an interested person called on the man who was selling the Aranda artists' paintings, ostensibly to buy. On the pretext of being unable to make up his mind, he persuaded the man to let him take some of the paintings away with him for careful perusal. He showed them to a member of the Arts Council in Hermannsburg together with a list of prices. One artist was questioned about a painting he recognised as his. It was priced at six guineas. The artist said the man in Alice Springs had paid him one and a half guineas. Other artists were also questioned and admitted selling their paintings cheaply. They were then warned that the man they were dealing with was dishonest, but it is still doubtful whether they really understood that they were being exploited. Mr. Oswald Wallent, the storeman at the Mission, was perturbed. He announced: 'The man who poses as a friend of the Aranda artists is definitely not an agent for the Hermannsburg Mission and his attempts at encouraging the artists are nothing short of an effort to wreck the honest intentions of the Mission to help the Arandas into a life of usefulness.'

In spite of efforts by Council members to prevent exploitation, the self-styled 'agent' continued to attract the gullible artists with hard cash-on-the-spot for their paintings. Although Albert Namatjira himself had no more dealings with the man, the unchecked exploitation was eventually to involve him.

Meanwhile he worked towards his ninth city exhibition, which was mounted in the Athenaeum Gallery, Melbourne, in November, 1948. It was yet another sell-out: 46 paintings, at from 18 to 55 guineas, yielded £1,519. The critics who claimed Albert was a 'freak' could no longer pursue this line because his three elder sons, Enos, Oscar and Ewald, had also become successful watercolourists and the two younger, Keith and Maurice, were showing talent for drawing. The three Pareroultja brothers also showed unusual talent in one family. Edwin and Otto achieved exhibitions in Melbourne, Sydney and Perth. The Melbourne and Sydney Art Galleries each purchased one of Edwin's paintings while ignoring Namatjira. Edwin's style has been likened by Rex Battarbee to that of Gauguin, while Otto's resembled Van Gogh's, yet neither had seen any of the work of these European masters. Ewald Namatjira also has a distinctive style. He achieves striking effects with colours inspired by traditional native art materials—brilliant ochres, clays and charcoals. As a child, Ewald was delicate and consequently had little education but his painting was remarkably mature by the time he was seventeen.

Ewald's promise was seriously set back by an accident. In July, 1949, while on a painting trip with his father, he decided to go hunting. His rifle accidentally discharged while he was chasing a kangaroo and the bullet entered his right eye and lodged near his brain. Albert took him to the Mission Hospital and from there he was flown to Alice Springs by the Royal Flying Doctor Service. Although Ewald lost the sight of his eye and the bullet could not be removed, he recovered quickly.

Albert, Rubina and the other sons often came to see him in hospital. The battered utility truck with 'ALBERT NAMAT-JIRA, ARTIST' painted on the driver's door, would pull up outside and, with Albert in the lead, would solemnly file into the ward bringing small gifts.

By 1949, Albert had become a man of such means that he began to think of investment. He set his mind on leasing 460 square miles of grazing land near Hermannsburg on which he hoped to establish a small cattle station. The ambition to own a cattle station was one more indication of his trend towards the status of a white man. He consulted Pastor Albrecht, pointing out that it would be a permanent investment from which his sons would benefit. He would build a home for himself and Rubina on the station and continue painting, leaving his sons to manage it. Pastor Albrecht

54

agreed that it was a good idea but warned Albert to make sure there was a permanent supply of water on the land.

The Senior Director of Native Affairs in Alice Springs, Mr. W. McCoy, commended Albert for his initiative; the granting of a grazier's licence could be in line with the policy of encouraging the aborigines to accept civic rights and responsibilities. So Albert applied to the Native Affairs and Lands Department for a grazier's licence as a preliminary to taking out a pastoral lease which would have to be renewed annually but which would make Albert virtually the owner of the land.

Everything seemed settled. But, while Albert was negotiating for the purchase of cattle, he was told that since a survey had failed to reveal a reliable source of water on the property his application for a grazier's licence must be refused. Albert was greatly disappointed but did not abandon hope. He decided to go to Darwin and personally put his case to officials there.

In July, 1950, Albert, and the late Bill Harney, well known Northern Territory identity, made the 1,000-mile journey to Darwin by motor coach. This was the farthest Albert had been from his tribal country and it was his first visit to anything like a town. If the curious stares of his fellow travellers embarrassed Albert, he did not show it. His composure remained unshaken even when, during the stop at the Daly Waters Hotel, the proprietor asked him to sign the visitors' book and a bystander, apparently under the impression that all aborigines communicated by smoke signals or message sticks, exclaimed: 'Good heavens, he can write!'

Albert ignored the remark. Bill Harney said that Albert's behaviour on the journey was a credit to the Hermannsburg missionaries. His dignity never forsook him.

Albert went straight to the Native Affairs Branch and Lands Department in Darwin to apply again for a grazier's licence. Although a decision could not be given immediately, the Administrator of the Northern Territory, Mr. A. R. Driver, promised to give the matter full consideration.

While in Darwin Albert decided to paint the scenery that was in such contrast to that of Central Australia. He was especially fascinated by the ocean, which he saw for the first time in his life. It presented a challenge to his skill. He tasted the water that foamed at his feet and was surprised to find it salty.

'It's not good to drink,' he said, 'but I think it will be good to paint.'

One can only imagine Albert's feelings as he stood looking at the vast expanse of water, for water was scarce in his tribal country and never found in large bodies. When he sat down to paint he found it difficult to capture the flat, subdued scene, so colourless after the magnificent mountain landscapes to which he was accustomed. His first attempt did not satisfy him so he promptly destroyed it. The next pleased him and he went on to paint three more scenes. A representative of the magazine, *The Australian Women's Weekly*, bought two for reproduction, a Darwin resident bought one, and Albert took the other back to Alice Springs.

The people of Darwin welcomed Albert. There was no evidence of colour prejudice; in fact, he was treated as a celebrity. He was the first full-blooded aborigine to dine in the exclusive Hotel Darwin and many prominent citizens were eager to meet him. He was invited to inspect H.M.A.S. Koala, which was in port, and the captain personally showed him around. This was something far beyond Albert's experience, either real or imagined. The engine room, especially, fascinated him.

Shopping where there was such a variety of unfamiliar merchandise also proved an exciting experience—and a costly one! Albert generously bought presents for 'all my family alonga back home', without keeping a tally of the cost. As a result, he had no money for his return to Alice Springs. However, Douglas Lockwood, a writer who had previously met Albert at Hermannsburg, heard of his plight and came to the rescue. When Albert returned to Hermannsburg he sent a cheque to Lockwood in repayment of the loan.

Namatjira's news value continued unabated. In June, 1950, two popular Australian magazines, *Pix* and *People*, published articles that were outspoken in their criticism of Australia's neglect of its aborigines. The article in *People* was the longest ever devoted exclusively to an aborigine and covered Namatjira's life from the time he began to work on the Hermannsburg Mission to his phenomenal success. It also referred to the several attempts to exploit him and aired some unpalatable facts as well as commenting on the fact that he had to pay income tax while being denied the normal privileges of the Australian citizen.

This, and similar articles, began to needle the public conscience. In an article published prior to Albert's second Sydney exhibition, author Colin Simpson wrote: 'Albert Namatjira is a signpost on the road to a new understanding by us of the capabilities of the aboriginal Australian. This was Namatjira's country before it was mine, yet I am a full Australian socially and he is not. But I regard it as an honour to open the exhibition of the paintings by Albert Namatjira.'

It almost goes without saying that this second Sydney exhibition—in Anthony Hordern's Gallery of Fine Arts — was a complete success. More than 500 attended the opening and so great was the rush to buy that the gallery manager was unable to control the crowd. Thirty-five of the 41 paintings were sold for 1,500 guineas within minutes of the opening. Individual prices ranged from 20 to 65 guineas.

The art critics were generally kinder but there was still a note of condescension. One review implied that Namatjira was a current craze and only time would prove whether his paintings would hold their value.

With the proceeds from his latest exhibition, Albert decided to buy a caravan. His application for a grazier's licence had finally been refused by Darwin and this was a big disappointment. Meanwhile, he had sold the house he had built and bought an Army disposals hut which had been re-erected near the main Mission buildings. His pride in his own home had been superseded by the memory of sorrow. His two daughters, Hazel and Martha, had died—Hazel at Hermannsburg in May, 1949, and Martha at Haast's Bluff in January, 1950. Since their deaths, Albert and Rubina had become very restless, spending less time at the Mission and more time on walkabout in Albert's beloved painting grounds. So Albert asked the Mission pastors for advice about buying a caravan. Both he and Rubina were getting old—Albert was now 48—and sleeping out in the cold desert nights was affecting their health. A caravan would also provide protection for his completed paintings when he was away from the Mission for long periods.

The pastors began negotiations for a caravan in September and a few weeks later Albert was delighted to see his new mobile home towed into Hermannsburg. He immediately attached it to his truck, loaded supplies, and left with Rubina on another painting walkabout.

Albert returned to Hermannsburg for the wedding of his former tutor Rex Battarbee and Miss Bernice Loone. The ceremony took place in the old Mission church and many natives, including the Aranda artists, were in the congregation. Among the wedding gifts displayed at the Superintendent's home were paintings from Albert and his sons and leather work by aboriginal craftsmen.

Soon after his tutor's marriage, Albert told the missionaries of his intention to build a new home, this time in Alice Springs. He had already arranged to buy a block of land. Battarbee was now Albert's agent and Albert thought he should be near him. Besides, 'it would be nice to live alonga house same as Mr. Battarbee.'

The missionaries explained that Albert might not be allowed to build a house in the town because aborigines were prohibited from remaining within the town boundaries after dark and advised him to enquire into the matter more fully before he took any action. But Albert, disregarding their advice, went ahead and finalised negotiations with a local business man for a building block on the west side of the town.

In March, 1951, the Press reported the sale. Albert's intention to build a house in Alice Springs created an unprecedented problem for the Northern Territory Administration; it was the first time an aborigine had sought to live in the town. Some white residents raised objections, arguing that if Albert had a town house, his many tribal relatives would also move in and become a nuisance. However, Mr. P. J. Rice, Albert's solicitor, counter-argued that if he had a home in the town, he would not be troubled by his many relatives and friends, who were becoming a serious drain on his finances. In fact, Albert was paying up to £80 a week for provisions for as many as 50 relatives with whom, under tribal law, he was obliged to share all he had.

While the Administrator of the Northern Territory was considering the case, Albert conferred with an architect on the design of a house to be built of stone or cement.

The progress of Albert's efforts to get the right to live in Alice Springs was given prominence in the national Press. Letters poured in from members of the public sympathising with him. A typical one appeared in the Brisbane *Courier Mail* under the heading: 'Let's give Albert a fair go.' 'There is still a good deal to be done by the people of Australia before it can be said with honesty, "We have given the natives a fair go",' wrote this correspondent. 'All Albert Namatjira, the full-blooded aboriginal artist, wants is a chance to settle down among white people in a small Australian town. This Australian native (more Australian by rights than the descendants of the settlers from the British Isles) has more rights to a home among the whites than many of our own members who don't contribute to art or culture, but merely regulate unproductively. Namatjira deserves more than he humbly seeks. Let him have it!'

There was a great deal of indignation among Australians generally, when it was announced on 20 April that the Administrator had decided not to grant the transfer of the building block. A site on a reserve near the town which was offered as a substitute was rejected.

Albert, at this time, was living in a crude hut he had built of bags and old iron at Morris Soak, a small waterhole several miles from Alice Springs. He was bitterly disappointed by the Administrator's decision. Morose and dejected, he seldom spoke to the companions who were camped with him. Then, after a few weeks at Morris Soak, he went back to Hermannsburg. He showed little interest in an exhibition of paintings held in Rex Battarbee's home in May, even though several of his water colours were included.

This exhibition had a special importance, for it presented works by no fewer than 13 aboriginal artists—the four Namatjiras (Albert, Enos, Oscar and Ewald), three Pareroultja brothers (Edwin, Otto and Reuben), Walter Ebatarinja, Henoch and Herbert Raberaba, Adolf and Gerhard Inkamala and Richard Moketarinja. Paintings by six white artists were also on show—Sidney Nolan, John Eldershaw, David M. Chittleborough, Les Turnbull, John A. Gardner and Rex Battarbee.

Despite the remoteness and smallness of Alice Springs, more than 500 people attended the opening by Mr. J. Nelson, M.H.R. Among the guests was the Governor of the Commonwealth Bank. Albert's lack of interest in the exhibition was understandable. Although his success had made him wealthy, he was becoming increasingly aware that, because he was an aborigine, he was not entitled to the same privileges as the white citizen. He was confused and unhappy about his status and bewildered by the laws of a civilisation he did not understand.

Namatjira's status as an Australian was also causing increasing public resentment against his treatment. The refusal of a grazier's licence and of the right to build a home in Alice Springs particularly rankled.

Although the Press had devoted much space over the years to Namatjira's work and such controversial issues as his merits as an artist and his social status, little had been published about his private life. This prompted Pastor Albrecht to write a pamphlet, *Albert Namatjira, Native Artist*. Its opening paragraph ran: 'For some years now, literature has been accumulating about Albert Namatjira, and, from a purely artistic point of view, newspapers particularly have glamorised him like a movie celebrity. In this article I shall try to avoid repetition of what has been written by others in order to show his background and the man as he is known here at the Mission Station.'

In addition to an account of Albert's youth, his work on the Mission and his development as an artist, Pastor Albrecht pointed out that Albert's growing wealth resulted in unconscious extravagance that caused constant concern. In spite of his large income, he was frequently insolvent. Then he had to wait until his latest exhibition refilled his empty bank account. Albert did not squander his money—he neither drank nor gambled—but his finances were drained by the persistent demands for luxuries by the large number of his tribal relations.

'Within the organisation of our Mission,' wrote the Pastor, 'Albert, as a capitalist, has become a serious problem. As has happened on a number of occasions, he will collect up to fifteen men and take them to town. They will enjoy his lavish hospitality, forgetting about work and other matters which have a claim on us in our daily life. While in town they establish contact with all sorts of undesirables, which has been the ruination of others.'

Various means had been employed to help Albert control his careless spending, but he used his chequebook regardless of his bank balance. The committee that guarded his interests had suggested that his cheques should have the counter signature of one of the committee. Albert had agreed to this for a while; and weekly or monthly sums were paid to him on a pre-arranged scale. But this restriction had, in practice, proved irksome, so Albert had requested that it be dropped.

Pastor Albrecht summarised the difficulty thus: 'Albert is

only one generation removed from real bush life where his ancestors used to roam about as nomads without any worldly possessions whatsoever. Closely connected with this is the complete lack of thought to hold on to what he has. He enjoys spending and likes a quick turnover. His father and forefathers never owned anything; why should he find enjoyment in keeping his possessions?'

The pamphlet concluded: 'Albert Namatjira, largely through his skill and determination, has become firmly established as a great artist and his name is written among the most prominent men of our time. He is the first aborigine to show what wonderful latent talent there is to be found among them. Through his income he has access to many things even the vast majority of white people cannot afford. Yet essentially he has remained a restless nomad; his greatest contentment comes to him when he is on the move, "walk-about", even if this means riding, as he usually does, right on the back of his truck, sitting hard on the boards of the tray over the back axle. In spite of his achievements, the tragedy of the Australian aborigine hangs over him; he has not found his level in our community in which, essentially, he has remained a stranger. Looking into the future, we cannot conceal a great amount of apprehension; he would have gained very little if through the dazzling lights of publicity and wealth he should lose himself—a wanderer between two worlds.'

This pamphlet was extensively distributed. While most readers agreed with the Pastor, there was some criticism—and this came from unexpected sources. Rex Battarbee was one who disagreed with his apprehension over Namatjira's future. He said: 'I do not think there is any danger of Namatjira being lost between native and white civilizations. He is essentially an aborigine, although a superior aborigine.'

This was the first time that a difference of opinion between Albert's two oldest friends had appeared in the Press but it was not, in fact, the first time there had been disagreement. For some months previously, Pastor Albrecht had been concerned with suggestions that Albert's affairs were not being managed satisfactorily. In addition, there were rumours that the Mission was 'lining its pockets'. The truth was that, until 1943, the sales were handled without any commission charges. Then 5 per cent and later 10 per cent commission was charged to cover costs of arranging exhibitions, framing of paintings, freight, etc., which was more than reasonable in the circumstances.

Because rumour was casting a slur on the Mission, it was considered advisable to sever art connections with Albert. Pastor Albrecht invited Rex Battarbee and the Superintendent of Native Affairs to Hermannsburg and told them that Albert's advisers at the Mission had decided, in view of these discrediting insinuations, to relinquish their offices. This would allow control of Albert to be taken over by those who sought it. The result was that the Aranda Arts Council was formed under the chairmanship of Rex Battarbee. The rift between Albert's friends widened and for some time it was widely publicised.

5

F OR a year or more, Albert was out of the public eye, with no exhibitions, no controversies and no disputes to rage about his uncomprehending head. But Rubina came into the news when the Adelaide *Mail* reported at length an interview with her.

'Being the wife of one of Australia's most colourful and famous artists does not mean a thing to Mrs. Namatjira,' wrote L. L. Whitelock. 'Life for her has hardly changed.'

The article described Rubina, squatting cross legged, native fashion, in a circle with other aboriginal women. The animated chatter was suddenly silenced by shyness as the interviewer approached. Rubina, asked if she was proud of Albert, replied casually: 'It's all right. Me likem.' Asked to pose for a photograph, she said: 'You no take me. Take Albert.' But Albert was away painting, so Rubina was persuaded to pose for a photograph with her granddaughter, Biddy, who had been with her ever since the little girl's mother had died. It was pointed out that Namatjira had no home of his own and that his wife sat in the dust outside a crude shanty.

These conditions in which Albert and his family lived were also noted by others. Dr. Darcy Morris, M.S.C., of Sydney, visiting Alice Springs as the guest of Father J. Tierney, M.S.C., the Catholic parish priest there, asked to meet Albert. Albert's camp was on the outskirts of the town. He himself was living in a wurlie of tree boughs, old bags and rusty galvanized iron. Father Tierney described the visit thus:

> As we approached the primitive dwelling, Dr. Morris remarked: 'Surely Albert doesn't live in there!' But sure enough, Albert emerged a few moments later in answer to my call, 'Are you there, Albert?' Dressed in old patched clothes, and wearing a battered army slouch hat, Albert was carrying a billy can of tea. We spent a good half hour in conversation together, Albert courteously and pleasantly answering the many questions Dr. Morris asked him. On the way back to the Presbytery, the Doctor remarked, 'There is a perfect example of the old saying, geniuses are born, not made.'

Father Tierney had come to know Albert well.

> I often met Albert when he came to see his friends. He was a most impressive personality, possessing a natural dignified bearing and a very placid temperament. His voice, deeply resonant, was pleasant to listen to when he spoke. He was not a 'talkative' type, but expressed his ideas clearly and simply. He always seemed pleased to answer any questions about his painting and his people, the Arandas. One of the most pleasant memories of my stay in Alice Springs will always be that I had the privilege of meeting and knowing Albert Namatjira.

Most people who met Albert were impressed in the same way. A visiting American, Mr. Vincent A. Hardy, who referred to the famous aboriginal as 'an unhappy child of Destiny', said he had been much perturbed to find him living in squalid conditions and also to learn that there were questionable dealings in his paintings and even rumours of a lucrative black market.

Early in 1952 it was evident that tourists in Alice Springs were buying paintings at high prices from dealers who

shrewdly concealed their identity. The Aranda Arts Council
and the Native Affairs Department were deeply concerned.
Of even greater concern was a suspicion that some of the
paintings were not genuine. Some, ostensibly under Albert's
signature, lacked the fine detail for which he was famous and
were otherwise definitely inferior, although they cleverly
imitated Albert's style. Rex Battarbee and Gordon Simpson,
a member of the Aranda Arts Council and a sub-agent, en-
deavoured unsuccessfully to discover the source of the faked
paintings. Albert himself showed little interest in the matter.
He had not recovered from the bitter disappointment of the
refusal of a permit to build a home in the town. He had
become more and more morose, avoiding contact with members of the council and acquaintances. Most of the time he
camped with his tribal relatives some miles out from Alice
Springs. But apparently he was still painting industriously
because he produced a good range of landscapes for an
exhibition at Anthony Hordern's Gallery in Sydney.

This exhibition in April, 1952, was not exclusively a Namatjira show. Seven Aranda artists were represented and the
competition for their work was not far short of that for the
Namatjiras because within half an hour 30 of the 57 paintings
were sold. By the end of the day, only four remained unsold.
Prices ranged up to 75 guineas. Mr. A. K. Marsden, director
of the Gallery, said: 'We could have sold three times the
number of paintings on show. The public likes aboriginal art.
All kinds of people bought the paintings—foreign consuls,
overseas airlines companies and local art connoisseurs.'

The paintings by Cordula Ebatarinja, the first Aranda
woman to become an artist, attracted particular interest. Her
style of art was quite different from that of her husband,
Walter, who had taught her to paint. But some art critics
would not admit, even after 14 years of successful exhibitions
by Namatjira, that aborigines could paint as well as white
artists. Isla Brooks, writing in the Sydney Survey column of
this controversy, commented that the tone of critics varied
from the loftily patronising to frankly unkind, but the over-

whelming sales success of the exhibition undoubtedly spoke for itself.

'We hope this success pleases the artists back there in the Centre. It certainly irritates some critics here,' she added.

Perhaps this comment was levelled at the National Gallery in Sydney, which had refrained from acquiring any Namatjira works, although State Galleries in three other capital cities had done so.

Six months after the Sydney exhibition, Mr. and Mrs. Battarbee staged an exhibition of Namatjira's paintings in their home. Alice Springs people bought £800 worth of paintings and £200 worth were acquired by interstate buyers. The highest-priced painting was 100 guineas. The outstanding work in this collection and the largest ever painted by Albert—it measured 34 inches by 18 inches—was of Mount Hermannsburg with the Mission nestling below its vividly coloured contours. This had been painted when Albert had gone to the Mission at the request of the Superintendent, who was worried about the artist's abandoned caravan at Haast's Bluff Native Reserve. Since his break with the Mission his visits there had been rare.

Battarbee considered the work in this exhibition the best Albert had ever done. The quality and the prices of the paintings shown should have discouraged people from buying the inferior black-market pictures that apparently bore Namatjira's signature, but the market continued to flourish. When Battarbee was in Adelaide for another exhibition in November, he told a reporter that paintings under the forged signatures of Albert Namatjira and other Aranda artists had been detected.

'I am certain someone is forging signatures,' he said. 'Some of the forgeries have been discovered in Melbourne and Adelaide. Adelaide police investigated the trouble two years ago. A man was questioned but no arrest was made. I have an idea who the guilty person might be, but it is hard to prove anything definite.'

Battarbee added that he had seen some work allegedly

done by Namatjira and the signature had obviously not been painted by him.

'Anyone who buys a painting by an Aranda artist painted in the last two or three years which does not bear the stamps on the back (that is, the official stamps of the Aranda Arts Council and Department of Native Affairs) runs the risk of buying a forgery. This sort of thing happens with all great art. Others try to cash in on it,' said Battarbee.

The new exhibition, in the Royal South Australian Society of Arts Gallery, showed paintings by Namatjira and two of the Pareroultja brothers. Albert's paintings sold at from 45 to 75 guineas, Edwin's and Otto's at from 7 to 20 guineas.

The success of the exhibition did nothing to lift Albert's spirits. Nor was he worried by the exposure by his agent of faked Aranda paintings. His sole interest lay in his plan to visit Western Australia. He had told few people of this project and, for many, the first intimation was an article by Eric Charles in *The West Australian* which announced that Albert intended to visit Perth early in the New Year (1953).

'Namatjira's decision,' the article said, 'is the result of a long emotional battle which reached a crisis with the latest refusal of the authorities to let him build a house and a studio in the Alice Springs "white area". Said Albert, "I'm sick of not being able to do what I like and go where I like. I earn my money like a white man and pay my taxes. Why can't I spend like a white man?" Namatjira's round dark face is inscrutable when he talks of his battles with officialdom, but underneath he is very sore. He will have to get the Native Affairs Department's permission for his visit to Perth, because as a full blood he is legally a ward and cannot travel outside the Northern Territory.'

The news launched more arguments and there was inexplicable opposition to his making the trip. The outcome was that he did not go. The reason was never made public and it was more than a year before he travelled beyond Northern Territory borders.

With yet another disappointment added to his burden,

Albert left Alice Springs for a while. While he was away, the scandal of the faked paintings broke out again. Police investigations had failed to find sufficient evidence that Albert's signature was being forged, so the Aranda Arts Council took the initiative. When Albert returned, he was asked to examine a painting bearing his name but which was signed in a manner different from the block capitals with which he always signed his work. Albert signed a statement that neither the painting nor the signature was his.

Newspapers all over Australia, and in some overseas countries, seized on the sensation. One report stated that many faked Namatjira paintings had been "peddled" in the south during the past twelve months. Another report claimed that numbers of faked Namatjira paintings had been located in South Australia and a man known to the police was alleged to have sold paintings purporting to be Namatjira's and other Aranda artists' works for 30 guineas. This man was believed to have conducted many previous dealings with the artists.

Many people who had bought Namatjira paintings now began to doubt their authenticity. Art dealers became wary and bought only paintings officially stamped, which caused further difficulties because none of the Aranda work painted before 1951 was stamped.

The 'Case of the Faked Paintings' as it was referred to affected many people, even a foreign diplomat in Melbourne who became suspicious of the authenticity of two paintings he contemplated buying. Before final settlement was made he had to fly to Alice Springs on official business, so he took the paintings with him. In Adelaide, *The News* reported: 'Australian artist and leader of the Aranda Arts Council took one look at the paintings and said: "These are both fakes. Albert Namatjira did not paint them. In fact, one is a copy of a fake."'

Another report quoted Battarbee as saying that although Albert Namatjira could write he did not sign his name on his paintings calligraphically nor did he sign them simply 'Namatjira'.

The *Australasian Post* published a two-page article by Alan Wauchope, entitled 'Take a Good Look at Your Namatjira — Maybe it's Not.' Wauchope wrote: 'Police and others are trying hard to pin down the author of the frauds. It will be a hard task, because under the law the perpetrator could easily escape on a technical point such as whether the signatory to the painting was a painter or merely his agent (and thus entitled to sign) or more significantly in this particular case whether the painter himself was legally entitled to write his name. This point immediately raised the question of Albert Namatjira's official status. Most white Australians regarded the dark Australians as not being entitled to any official status. Under the Northern Territory Aboriginal Ordinance, coloured native Australians were not able to vote or drink intoxicating liquor and did not receive social services and were prohibited from living in the town area of either Darwin or Alice Springs, but were subject to all other laws of the Commonwealth, including income tax. The widespread publicity given to the case of forgeries of Albert Namatjira's paintings prompted some questioning of the status of the aborigine who had, through his art, become famous and successful. The artist himself appeared unconcerned over all the fuss about forgeries of his paintings. He had been called upon to sign a statement that one particular painting was not his and neither was the signature his and had expressed the opinion "that there had been too much fuss made and he wasn't worried about forgeries, he could paint plenty more pictures".'

Interest in the allegations of faked Namatjiras intensified as newspapers gave prominence to each new development. Then came an unexpected and dramatic climax. From Alice Springs it was reported that paintings with Namatjira's signature were being held by the police. The paintings had been found among the personal possessions of a middle-aged man who had died in the town. A solicitor emphasises it was the normal practice for police to hold all belongings of a deceased person until such were claimed by relatives. However, members of the Aranda Arts Council were summoned to inspect the paintings. They bore no official stamps and Namatjira's name was signed diagonally across the bottom of each one.

Albert inspected five of these paintings and said he had never printed his name diagonally. He added: 'I have never seen these paintings before.' Mr. Gordon Simpson, in his official capacity as a member of the Aranda Arts Council inspected the paintings at the Police Station and said the signature diagonally across the bottom right hand corner was definitely not in accordance with Albert's practice of signing his name.

'As a sub-agent,' he said, 'I have handled much of his work and have never seen a genuine Namatjira painting with his name signed diagonally. The paintings I inspected at the Police Station appeared to be clever copies of Albert's style and only an expert would recognize that these were copies.'

It was assumed that police action would follow and there was some dissatisfaction when it was not forthcoming. Finally, a spokesman for the Aranda Arts Council suggested that the police should re-open their investigations into faked Namatjira landscapes sold in the southern States during 1953.

A report in *The News*, Adelaide, on 14 January 1954, stated: 'Last year police investigated three fakes sold for 40 and 50 guineas in South Australia. After that, the police of the Northern Territory, South Australia and Victoria seemed to wipe their hands of the matter. The Council believes the faker is still at large, carrying on a lucrative business. It warns the public not to buy any paintings not bearing the special stamps of the Council and the Native Affairs Branch, with the initials of the officers.'

This report was the last public reference to illicit dealings in faked Namatjira paintings. The extent to which events of those months affected Albert could not be gauged by his

manner. Naturally reticent, he appeared — outwardly, anyway — to accept adverse incidents and the failure of cherished
ambitions with the same equanimity that he accepted fame
and its attendant distinctions; he had, for instance, shown
little enthusiasm when he heard he had been awarded the
Queen's Coronation Medal. His first knowledge of this had
come when he and his sons were painting at the Haast's Bluff
Native Reserve. Sydney author, Frank Clune, was visiting
them. Clune had a radio. While listening to a broadcast on
Coronation eve, Albert heard that he, together with other
distinguished Australians, had been honoured by the Queen
with the bestowal of medals to commemorate her Coronation.
Albert had little to say; he was more interested in planning
some landscapes for Clune. Clune took back to Sydney four
paintings — all of the same scene. But each was a different
interpretation. They had been painted by Albert and his
three sons, Enos, Oscar and Ewald, each in his individual
style.

While Albert was at Haast's Bluff, he discovered a copper
deposit on the Areyonga Native Reserve. He pegged a claim
and applied to have it assayed. But once again Albert's hopes
foundered; the rock was very hard and yielded only 27% ore
— not enough to make mining profitable. Albert's failure in all
his ventures outside painting troubled his friends at Hermannsburg; they noticed, on his rare visits to the Mission,
that he had changed a great deal. He confessed that his fruit-
less efforts to better himself had made him very unhappy.
He also told the missionaries that since he had left the
Mission to live near his agent in Alice Springs, his financial
liabilities had increased because many of his kinsmen had
followed and set up camp with him. There were about 50
of them and if he did not buy them all they demanded, they
went into town and bought goods, booking them to his
account. He also had to pay for frequent repairs to his truck,
which was driven by any of his tribesmen who could drive.

It was apparent that Albert was finding it difficult to
manage his affairs without the guidance and advice that had

been his while he lived at Hermannsburg. Under the burden of his personal problems, Albert was only casually interested in an invitation to Canberra to be presented to the Queen during the forthcoming Royal Tour.

6

WHILE the Commonwealth was eagerly looking forward to the Royal Tour early in 1954, Namatjira was preparing for his visit to Canberra and for a tour of Sydney, Melbourne and Adelaide, cities he would be seeing for the first time. He had been advised that the Northern Territory Administration had made all arrangements, including the ordering of suits and accessories to be picked up when he arrived in Darwin. However, Albert wanted to be smartly dressed for his journey north so he bought a new outfit before he left Alice Springs.

On the morning of his departure, on 3 February, he called on his friends, Mr. and Mrs. Ralph Tuncks, whose store he often patronized. Mrs. Tuncks commented on his smart appearance, then noticed his shoes were dusty. She offered polish and brushes. Albert, unaccustomed to having anyone notice his appearance, was flattered by this interest and promptly polished his shoes till they shone. Then he stood back for final approval.

'I look all right now, you think?' he asked. 'Then I go. That plane wait to fly me alonga Darwin.'

With a warm handshake he walked proudly out of the shop.

This was to be Albert's first flight, but he showed no signs of apprehension as he waited to board the aircraft. The Battarbee family and Alan Wauchope had come to see him off. Was he thrilled to be going to meet the Queen? Albert's face remained expressionless.

'Oh yes, I'm thrilled about everything,' he said. 'It's a great honour.'

Wauchope asked him if he was taking a present for the Queen and Albert replied quietly that it was not for private people to offer her gifts.

But Albert did have a painting for the Queen; he did not speak of it because he was vaguely aware of a thing called protocol. The Administrator of the Northern Territory, Mr. F. J. S. Wise, said: 'Albert was asked by Mr. McCaffery, Acting Director of Native Affairs, with my concurrence, to paint a very special picture for presentation to the Queen. Albert readily agreed but he would never have initiated such an idea.'

On the flight to Darwin, although this was a new experience, Albert had all the assurance of a seasoned air traveller. His main concern when he arrived at the airport was the white linen suits which had been made for him by a Chinese tailor. Douglas Lockwood, an old friend and admirer, was there to interview him about his presentation to the Queen and his first visit to the big cities.

Albert flew south in a Constellation airliner, accompanied by the Administrator, Mrs. Wise and other members of the Northern Territory delegation who were to be presented to the Queen. After arrival in Sydney, Australia's largest city with a population of 2,000,000, he was driven from the airport through the industrial area of Mascot.

'Do people really live here?' he asked.

The party were two hours in Sydney before continuing the journey to Canberra. Albert was not overawed by the Canberra Hotel. His deferential manner and innate sense of politeness did not waver under curious stares. On the morning of 15 February, Albert, in a white linen suit, joined the assemblage at Government House for presentation to the Queen and the Duke of Edinburgh. The pageantry of the occasion was given an exotic flavour by a detachment of the

75

Royal Papuan and New Guinea Constabulary, a Manus Island Naval detachment, and brass and pipe bands of the Pacific Islands Regiment.

'Among the many distinguished Australians presented to the Royal visitors, the tall, handsome, dark aboriginal artist was without a doubt the most outstanding personality,' wrote another guest. 'The Minister for Territories, the Honorable Paul Hasluck, presented Albert, who bowed with inborn grace to Her Majesty, then touched her proffered hand with his dark tapering fingers. The Royal dignity of the Queen and the natural dignity of the man descended from the oldest Australian race was an unforgettable spectacle. All those who witnessed this will always remember the charming smile with which Her Majesty greeted Albert Namatjira and the sincere friendliness with which Prince Philip added his own greeting.'

Namatjira was also invited to attend the State Ball in King's Hall, Parliament House, the most glittering social occasion in Australia's history. His introduction into white society was overwhelming; the crowds and ceremonies bewildered him.

On 18 February, Albert left for a week in Sydney as the guest of Frank Clune. Albert had hoped for relief in Sydney from the bewildering whirl that had swept him up in Canberra. He was disappointed. Namatjira had become almost a legend. Sydney knew his work but not the man. He would certainly not be allowed to hide away. Many social and public engagements had been arranged.

'Albert Namatjira, the Aranda artist, who to many Australians personifies the dignity of the aboriginal race, is now being initiated into the social ways of Sydney,' reported the *Sydney Morning Herald.* 'On Wednesday he attended an opening of an exhibition of newspaper art at the David Jones Gallery. On Wednesday evening he attended a party given in his honour at the Vaucluse home of Mr. and Mrs. Frank Clune, and at 3 p.m. yesterday he spoke at an exhibition of contemporary art at Anthony Hordern's Art Gallery. All this might well have flustered a man who has spent most of his life in the Aranda tribal country, an area of 1,000,000 acres near Alice Springs. But Mr. Namatjira weathered the crowd yesterday with his composure unshaken. He made his way through a crowd of 500 people to the dais and the Lord Mayor, Alderman P. D. Hills, made a speech declaring the exhibition open. At the Lord Mayor's invitation, Mr. Namatjira mounted the dais, stood before the microphone and said: "Well, ladies and gentlemen, I haven't been in a city before in my life. I think I have three times now had pictures coming on exhibition in this place here, and I am very pleased to thank you for being here." Albert Namatjira had scarcely finished speaking when the buying rush which had been a feature of all his previous exhibitions turned the crowd into a shambles.'

Some people, failing in their efforts to secure paintings, turned their attention to Albert as he sat at a table autographing catalogues. A mêlée developed as people elbowed their way to the table. *The Bulletin* reported: 'Several society ladies, unable to get near Namatjira for the throng, crawled on all fours to push their catalogues through to be autographed.' It was, said *The Bulletin*, a fantastic opening day, combining the social and artistic excitement of Dobell's recent show with the ferocity of a big store bargain sale opening.

'Of course, there is a lot of fashion in all this,' the report continued, 'and a lot of white artists are put in the very awkward position of having to be jealous of the patronage thus lavished on aborigines. But there is also a sense of history in it. There is no doubt about it, it's an artistic as well as an historical phenomenon, and though one does not want to overrate it, artistically it is really shocking that the New South Wales Gallery does not own a panel of these most interesting water colours and hasn't bothered to buy a Namatjira painting, but at Dobell's show the Trustees of the gallery spent over £500.'

This exhibition included twelve paintings by Namatjira

and the work of nine other Aranda artists, including the Pareroultja brothers, Walter Ebatarinja and his wife Cordula, Richard Moketarinja, Herbert Raberaba and Enos Namatjira. Albert Namatjira's paintings were sold for £600 and, as usual, were snapped up in minutes. The other 46 paintings were sold by the end of the second day.

After seven hectic days in Sydney, Albert was relieved to get on the train for Melbourne, saying as he did so: 'I get a rest now. Too much rush in Sydney, too many people.'

The Melbourne itinerary had been planned by a close friend of Albert's, Pastor Philip Scherer. The aim was to let Albert experience something of city life without the trying social and public functions that he had been plunged into in Sydney. But, despite the Pastor's precautions, Albert did became involved in two incidents. The police had to be summoned to control the crowds which mobbed Albert when he was walking in the street, taking his first real opportunity of seeing the bright lights of a big city. The second incident occurred when, at an exhibition of Australian art in the Town Hall, visitors crowded around begging autographs. After they had been brought under control, Albert continued his inspection of the paintings, ignoring the gaping crowd.

Albert's other engagements passed without incident. He particularly enjoyed a dinner given by the late J. K. Moir, a noted collector of Australiana. At the dinner he met many leading artists. He was also happy to attend a meeting of members of the Aborigines Welfare Board. He visited the beautiful orchard country around Doncaster, 12 miles out of Melbourne, went on a cruise of the River Yarra and was driven through the Dandenong Ranges where he inspected the well-known open-air gallery of William Ricketts, a sculptor who has devoted his latter life to the aborigines and to the interpretation of their life and legends.

On his visit to the Wycliffe Summer School of Linguistics Albert met Mr. Wilfred A. Douglas from Kalgoorlie, Western Australia, Superintendent of the United Australian Mission Languages Department.

'Before Albert arrived,' he said, 'I asked permission of the assembled company to address him in the Western Desert language. On being introduced to Albert, I asked him, "Nyuntulu wangka ninti?" (Do you know the language?) To which he immediately replied with a loud "Uwama" (Definitely, yes!) He then revealed to me that he had married a "desert" woman and could speak her language fluently. After the formal part of the meeting had concluded, Albert compared vocabulary items with me in Aranda and Pitjantjara. I supplied words in the latter while he gave me the equivalents in Aranda. He seemed to immensely enjoy this exercise and showed a real love for the native culture and language.'

Wherever Albert went in Melbourne, people were anxious to do what they could for him. When the two cars of his party arrived at the Shrine of Remembrance, there was not a parking space available except in a prohibited area. A patrolling policeman came up, saw the aborigine in one of the cars, and said to the driver, 'Is that Albert Namatjira?' The driver nodded. The policeman said, 'I'm a great admirer of Albert Namatjira. You can park here while he visits the Shrine.'

Albert made many new friends in Melbourne and won the admiration of all who met him.

Pastor Scherer, Albert's host, summed up his visit: 'Everywhere, Albert conducted himself admirably and was paid the greatest respect. Many requests had to be declined, as he already had a full programme. He received a large number of gifts, including a tent, a big flag, books, pottery, paints, clothes, photographs, etc. Generally considered, I believe he should benefit greatly from his new contacts. By casual remarks he showed he saw through anything undesirable and he took everything calmly.'

Albert travelled by train to Adelaide on 4 March and was met by Pastor M. Lohe, President General of the United Evangelical Church of Australia, and Dr. Charles Duguid, President of the Aborigines Advancement League.

Only two official functions were arranged for his stay in Adelaide — a reception by the Aborigines Advancement

League and a reception by the Royal South Australian Society of Arts. The Arts Society reception, out of courtesy to Albert who, by law, was prohibited from drinking alcohol, was 'dry.' Private engagements included a visit as the guest of Pastor and Mrs. R. B. Reuther, to Light's Pass, in the predominantly Lutheran Barossa Valley. Albert spoke to the children at the local school and answered questions. To their delight he sketched emus and kangaroos on a blackboard.

Pastor Reuther said later that Albert was very tired after his tour and added: 'I believe Albert found his first visit to the big cities interesting. Although he did not say very much, my wife and I got the impression that he had not liked being surrounded by so many people wherever he went. He said he missed his wife and family and was looking forward to returning to Central Australia. One morning Albert walked around our spacious flower garden in silent contemplation and I asked him what he thought of the beautiful Barossa Valley orchards and vineyards. His reply was a brief "Very nice," but I sensed he was thinking of his own beautiful country with its magnificent mountainous grandeur, and that he was longing to returning to it. Before he left us, Albert asked me for a loan of £20 as he wished personally to buy presents for his wife, Rubina, and his children. The loan was later repaid. All the time Albert was with us he behaved like a gentleman; his general manners were all that could be desired.'

Before he returned to Adelaide, Albert said he would like to call on his old friends, Mr. and Mrs. Heinrich, at Gawler, for he had been their driver on their memorable journey to Hermannsburg back in 1924 — a journey which Mrs. Heinrich always described as the most unusual honeymoon any bride ever had.

During a long talk with these old friends, Albert spoke of his mounting troubles in recent years. They asked if success and increasing income pleased him. He thought for a moment, then replied: 'I was happier before I was a rich man. Money is not everything.' He explained that money could not buy him what he most wanted, a home of his own in Alice Springs. Of his meeting with the Queen he said: 'She was a nice little *kwara kwaka* (little girl.)' When leaving, he told them he did not want to visit the big cities again; they were too noisy and there were too many people.

One of the happiest and proudest experiences of Albert's stay in Adelaide was being taken to the Adelaide National Art Gallery where the Director, Mr. Robert Campbell, showed him the painting the Gallery had bought at his first Adelaide exhibition in 1939. Albert said later that Melbourne and Sydney did not have any of his paintings, but he thought Melbourne would soon buy one because the Director had asked to see some for selection.

Albert returned to Alice Springs by train, accompanied by two of the Hermannsburg Mission staff. Throughout the thousand-mile journey, his one thought was of being reunited with his family. At Alice Springs Albert went straight to his camp to be heartily welcomed by his wife and, inevitably, a large number of tribal relations eager to discover what presents Albert had brought them from the great cities they had never seen.

7

FOR some months after his return, Albert worked on some landscapes, the best of which were sent to Mr. (later Sir) Daryl Lindsay, Director of the National Gallery in Melbourne. The Trustees wanted one example for their own collection and another for the Geelong Art Gallery. Three were chosen — by Rex Battarbee — and priced at 35, 50 and 75 guineas. The Gallery Trustees, however, rejected them. The Professor of Fine Arts at Melbourne University, Professor J. A. Burke, said: 'I think they are frightful. I think we should also state that we are going to look around for an early Namatjira. These are absolute pot-boilers.' The Chairman of the Trustees, Sir John Medley, said: 'I think we should write back saying that the price is too high and that Namatjira's work has gone downhill terribly.'

These comments brought an irate reply from Rex Battarbee who said, in a telephone interview from Alice Springs, that the paintings submitted to the Victorian Art Gallery were the best available examples of Namatjira's present work. Battarbee was reported by *The News*, Adelaide, as saying: 'If they want to say those things, it's a free country. But they don't know what they are talking about. They wanted cheaply priced pictures and we gave them the best work available at a reduced price. Albert is not painting pot-boilers. His work is equal to the best technique. What more can he do? He is not at all concerned whether the Gallery buys his pictures or not, but I would like to see it buy them. They had the chance to buy on the early market. Some of the early works have been resold for 200 guineas.'

Albert was not in Alice Springs when the argument raged. But when he was next in town he said he could not understand why they did not like his paintings. 'I think the paintings were good ones. They got them cheap because Mr. Lindsay told me when I was in Melbourne that he wanted a painting a little bit cheap.'

Critics of Albert's art included Robert Campbell, Director of the Adelaide National Gallery.

'Namatjira is undoubtedly a remarkable man,' he was reported as saying. 'But his rating as an artist is not particularly high. He is by no means a water colourist of the front rank. The extraordinary success he has had is because in Namatjira we have a full blooded aborigine who cannot only paint in the Western manner but can also see through the white man's eyes. There is no doubt whatsoever that Namatjira's paintings will be of considerable historical value as the old aboriginal art passes away with age-old culture. There is no reason why later on Australia should not produce a top-rank aboriginal artist.'

Campbell's suggestion that Australia might in time produce an outstanding aboriginal artist was widely argued. Many people believed that the art of the 'father' of the Aranda school of artists would never be surpassed. Some supporters even asserted that none of his critics would ever be as successful as Namatjira and that his paintings would hold their value long after their works were forgotten.

The controversy finally subsided. The much-discussed paintings were returned to Alice Springs and no more was heard about Professor Burke's suggestion that the Melbourne Gallery Trustees would 'look around for an early Namatjira.'

Although many authorities did not have a very high opinion of Namatjira's worth as an artist, the Royal Arts Society of New South Wales nevertheless considered him worthy of recognition and elected him an honorary member.

Albert was painting in Palm Valley at the time of his election. Mr. A. E. Williams, Manager of the Victorian Tourist Bureau in New South Wales, was deputed to take the news to Albert. He found Albert camped at one of his favourite painting sites. When told of the honour bestowed on him, Albert made no immediate comment. He thought for a while; then, with one of his rare smiles, said how pleased he was to hear that artists in New South Wales had honoured his work.

Reg Campbell, a New South Wales artist, sought permission to paint Albert's portrait during a visit to Central Australia. Mrs. Campbell, who accompanied her husband, said both she and her husband had long been interested in the aboriginal artist from newspaper and magazine articles they had read. But when they met him their preconceived ideas had to be amended.

Mrs. Campbell wrote: 'During the time Albert "sat" for his portrait, I felt I was privileged to discover much of the depths of this truly remarkable man's character as was humanly possible. He had great dignity and an astonishing knowledge of his own subject, watercolour painting, and of his fellow men — both dark and white. I talked with him at great length and he told me of many of his tribal laws and of his dealings and experiences with white people. I asked him how he first came to draw or paint. In his own broken English, Albert told me that as a young man he had been a keen walker and the walk into Alice Springs (80-odd miles) was just a short stroll. His long walks took him into wild, unknown country, to places where his tribe had never been. So as to show his people what he had seen, Albert told me: "I gettum broad bark. I gettum stick from fire. I draw hills, valleys, trees and rocks on bark. These I show my people." I asked him whether he still had any of these bark drawings, but he assured me that he had burned them as soon as he explained them. Albert also told me why so many of his people can draw. He explained that as there was no written language among the

Arandas they all, from an early age, draw anything they wish to convey to their companions. This I could understand as I have some drawings by aboriginal children and the most talented white children could not have expressed the same accuracy as these native children had done. Every picture appears to tell a story of what these little people saw yesterday or what they hope will happen tomorrow. Albert's explanation had helped me to see so clearly the inborn talent for art in our native Australians.

'Perhaps the most amusing incident connected with the painting of Albert's portrait was when we first approached him with the request. Albert agreed willingly to sit for my husband, but looked remorsefully at his tattered old shirt and remarked: "More better I have new red shirt." So we took him into the town. At the local store he chose a red shirt and a blue shirt and a green shirt. There was a moment of embarrassment when my husband realized he was to pay for the shirts. However, he did; but Albert still appeared to be disconsolate. It seemed his tribe of relatives would have to be kept happy while he sat for his portrait. "They would want a good meal of steak," said Albert. "More better if rump steak." By the time we finished shopping for Albert and his relatives it had cost us three new shirts, 100 rounds of ammunition for his sons to go shooting kangaroos, a case of lemonade for the children, £10 for Rubina and a generous helping of rump steak for every member in the camp. Yet, there had not been one atom of conniving or greed in Albert's suggestions that we buy all this, so we accepted the situation and loved him the more for it. We had seen a side of Albert that was all little boy. It was an uncommercial way of getting paid for something he had been asked to do.

'Another amusing incident, but one which my husband has rarely allowed me to recount, occurred during the sittings. I had prepared a meal for Albert and my husband and before serving it called my husband aside and told him to eat the steak with his fingers, as Albert and his people always did —

so I thought. After serving the meal I returned in a little while to find out if anything further was required and found my husband simply livid. He was eating his steak with his fingers whilst Albert had found a knife and fork and was using these with a refined elegance, holding them with natural grace in his sensitive, tapering fingers.

'Although the painting was begun at Albert's camp because we wanted him in his own surroundings, the situation became intolerable with many distractions, swarms of flies, innumerable dogs, piccaninnies, inquisitive relatives and the eternal red dust rising in clouds every time someone moved. So we persuaded Albert to come to the home of Mrs. Pat Davies where we posed him in the dining room and, to avoid a stiff studied pose, hung a water colour by Hans Heysen for him to look at. Albert sat relaxed, studying and analysing this painting, every now and again asking how certain colour effects had been obtained. Albert was truly interested and dedicated to art.

'For my husband and I, meeting and getting to know Albert Namatjira so well was one of the most memorable experiences in our lives. We found him to be a great man, both as an artist and as an Australian — a truly lovable and unforgettable character.'

That year, 1954, was the most eventful in Namatjira's life: he had been presented to the Queen and personally acclaimed in three capital cities. After 16 years, the almost legendary figure had become a public figure; and his debut into the social life of the cities had made him one of the most newsworthy Australians of the year. What would be his status as a citizen now? Many people believed he merited full citizenship rights which would entitle him to all the privileges enjoyed by white and part-coloured Australians. They were indignant that he should be prohibited from living in a home of his own in Alice Springs and that he was obliged to live outside the town boundaries in a squalid, unsanitary camp. People who had met him during his visit to the southern cities recalled his efforts to improve his living conditions, firstly by applying for a station property and then a home in Alice Springs — both of which had been refused by official rulings.

The bitter anomalies in Namatjira's standing as an Australian were emphasized by the news of his arrest on a charge of having drunk wine.

At the court hearing, evidence was given that an aboriginal and a half-caste had got drunk on wine. They offered Albert a drink. Albert, in his defence, claimed he had only sipped from the bottle to show he was friendly and to avoid unpleasantness, not because he was a drinker. The policeman who arrested Albert admitted that he was not under the influence of liquor and had not denied having a drink.

The presiding Magistrate, Mr. W. S. Nicholls, S.M., found the facts against Albert proved, but dismissed the case without a conviction, saying he felt that Namatjira had been the victim of circumstances. Questioned later, Albert was deeply distressed.

'My people not used to wine,' he said. 'In the old days there was never any trouble. The law says half-castes can drink, so they bring wine into camp, then everybody drinks. Then much trouble.'

Albert's arrest and appearance in court were prominently featured in newspapers throughout Australia. Controversy flared up again. Rex Battarbee challenged the Northern Territory laws.

'With all due respects to the Minister for Territories, Mr. Hasluck,' he said, 'I believe the full Citizenship Rights Bill for half-castes will be the downfall of the full-blood aborigines. Many so-called half-castes live with full-blood wives and other natives. Now they can go to hotels, buy wine and bring it to their homes, leading full-blood natives astray. Albert Namatjira is a rich man and when he sets up camp outside Alice Springs he is besieged by part aborigines and others whose only regard for their newfound freedom is to over-indulge in liquor.'

87

Battarbee added that in all the years he had known Albert, he had never seen him take intoxicating liquor.

Newspapers gave prominence to various facets of Albert's unique position. Several stressed the ancient aboriginal law of sharing all material possessions. By tradition, therefore, liquor must also be shared. The white man's law permitting part-aborigines to drink and prohibiting full-bloods from doing so was quite inexplicable to them.

The Sun, Melbourne, devoted almost half a page to Albert Namatjira's dilemma:

'Albert Namatjira has said little about the night he spent in a cell, but it is certain this experience has caused him to think about other things than painting. The white man's appreciation of his art lifted him from obscurity and placed him on a pedestal. Fame brought great riches and took him into the realms of white high society and endowed him with a rare, and even unique, honour, being presented to Her Majesty the Queen. And with these privileges and honours of civilization came also the "privilege" of contributing towards the upkeep of "his" country. The white man's law demanded that he should pay income tax for the earnings from his paintings, somewhere in the vicinity of £400 per annum on his reputed earnings of £2,000 or £3,000 annually. But he has been denied many other civilized privileges, the right to go where he wants to, the free right to purchase property. Namatjira is reported to have said, "My people are tired of walking around reserves like animals and living in tents like 'new' people."

'Yet the people who are most concerned with the welfare of the aborigines and their assimilation with civilized living agree that the law, which brought disgrace to a world-famed member of the native Australians, must be upheld. A free supply of intoxicating liquor to aborigines could cause havoc among these people to whom any form of alcohol is totally unknown. It could cause unprecedented behaviour that would be the greatest bar towards their assimilation. A permit for natives to drink would also bring about a grave exploitation by white men.

'Namatjira returned from his first taste of civilization apparently unimpressed with the glitter of this way of life. Gladly he returned to his own people; he had no desire to remain in the environment in which he had been "lionized." For Albert, the love and affection and esteem of his tribe meant more to him. Despite his fame he has never separated himself from his family. Except for his visit to cities he has always had some members of his family with him. Now, after his conviction, it is likely the white man's way of life will be even less important and his tribal life more important.'

Albert was so deeply affected by his appearance before a court that he separated himself completely from those associated with the charge. He left his camp near Alice Springs and spent most of the following twelve months in the isolated fastnesses of his tribal country beyond the Hermannsburg Mission. Occasionally he went in to Alice Springs to take paintings to Battarbee, but he avoided all contact with anyone connected with his disgrace.

The next year, 1955, was uneventful. Albert spent most of his time painting with other Aranda artists and was seldom seen, even at Hermannsburg. He was in the news only briefly — when some of his paintings were included in an exhibition of the works of twelve Aranda artists in Sydney. This exhibition was yet another success.

Ten years before, someone had pondered Namatjira's future. 'Will Fame, that fickle mistress, court and then defeat him?' Albert had indeed experienced the fickleness of fame. He had been defeated in his efforts to obtain the things he most desired. The rejection of his work by the Victorian and South Australian Galleries was a bitter disappointment.

For the first time, the word 'tragedy' appeared in a newspaper article referring to Namatjira's social status and his status as an artist. Under the headline, 'Black Artist and Tragic Dilemma,' *The Advertiser*, Adelaide, recounted the now-familiar facts about Albert's unhappy situation: 'Albert sits under a tree below Mount Gillen like a king, apart from his relations, a ragged and untidy lot. His own appearance is untidy yet commanding. These people are the remnants of a once-proud Aranda tribe, but pride is a thing of the past now.'

A spokesman for the Hermannsburg Mission, said: 'Albert's tragedy is that he is living between two worlds. He progressed beyond his simple way of life into a life of confusion in the commercial world of civilization. He left his own happy environment only to find he was not accepted by white society into which his artistic talent had projected him. Thus, unhappy and frustrated, he now lives between two societies, his own and that of civilization. Instead of the fulfilment of his hopes, Albert has found only frustration; instead of happiness he has found humiliation. His tribal laws demand that he shares all he has with his many tribal relations, his fame demands an ever increasing production of paintings. The tragedy of Albert Namatjira, a simple child of nature, is unfortunately only too common. The pathos of his story seems to be the rule rather than the exception whenever a member of the dark races attempts to enter white society.'

Albert's increasing unhappiness became apparent to the townspeople on his rare visits to Alice Springs. He seemed embittered, disillusioned, his quiet, pleasant manner replaced by an attitude of resentment towards everyone and everything.

8

EARLY in 1956 came rumours of a rift between Namatjira and his agent, Rex Battarbee. Namatjira had come to resent the Aranda Arts Council's restriction on his disposing of his paintings privately. He felt he should be free to sell to anyone he wished at prices he specified. Many sympathized with him on this point, even though they realized the Council had been set up to protect the Aranda artists from exploitation. Namatjira often sold his paintings to storekeepers and visiting tourists. However, he still took a certain amount of work to his agent, although he was dissatisfied with having to wait until it was sold before he received payment.

It was no surprise, then, when Battarbee announced that he was no longer acting as Namatjira's agent. He was quoted in *The News*, Adelaide, as saying: 'In the last year of my sole agency in Alice Springs for all native artists' work, including Namatjira's, I sold 1,034 paintings by 18 artists for about £7,600. I got 10% for my trouble and was happy to help them. But now unauthorized dealers want only Namatjira's work and Albert's contemporaries in Alice Springs are having a lot of trouble finding markets. Albert can't complain. With the demand for his work he could wait for top prices every time. But he seems to go on selling for whatever the first comer offers, then if he wants another few pounds the next day, he can always hustle off something, even if it is only a pot boiler.'

Battarbee also alleged that some unauthorized dealers in Alice Springs made up to 400% on paintings by Namatjira and other aboriginal artists. Namatjira himself asserted that one painting in an Alice Springs shop window with a price tag around the £90 mark was one he sold for £20. Battarbee also said a tourist had bought seven paintings from Namatjira for a total of £100. Their true value was nearer £400.

The Northern Territory Legislative Council became so concerned by reports of exploitation of the Aranda artists that it amended the Police Offences Act and instituted a £100 fine or six months' gaol or both for the buying of native paintings direct without the permission of the Native Affairs Branch in Alice Springs. In spite of this, the illegal traffic continued. It was believed that paintings were being sent to Sydney, where there was an enormous demand, especially for Namatjiras.

When the illegal traffic made news, the Native Affairs Branch came under fire for its failure to apprehend the unauthorized dealers. One reporter went to Alice Springs and found Namatjiras openly on sale in shops at 80 to 100 guineas. When Battarbee was interviewed he said he was tired of spendthrift artists who earned and squandered small fortunes. His own work had suffered because he had spent so much time acting as agent, so he had severed his connection with the native artists.

Next came a report that Albert was destitute. The Director of Native Affairs, Mr. H. Giese, announced that Namatjira was seriously in debt. At one stage it looked as if a writ would have to be issued to recover a car he owned. A spokesman at the Hermannsburg Mission disclosed that during one of Albert's rare visits he appeared worried and admitted he owed large sums to stores and garages in Alice Springs. Albert's main concern was that frequent repairs to his truck had cost several hundred pounds which he had been unable to pay and that the truck was still in a garage for additional repairs. Consequently he had to hire taxis. He had actually taken a taxi to Hermannsburg. The fare was £15!

While Albert had been at the Mission, major expenditure was supervised by the staff. Until 1951 he had never been seriously in debt; in fact, savings invested in War Bonds amounted to £900. But after he left the Mission he bought a three-ton, four-wheel-drive truck at an exorbitant price, a half-ton utility and a second-hand car in poor condition. Since Albert seldom drove himself, these vehicles were driven over rough country by any member of his tribe who could drive. Repairs were frequent and costly.

The death of Albert's father, Jonathan, in March, 1956, had affected him deeply, even though for some years he had not seen much of him. Jonathan, one of the first Aranda converts to the Lutheran faith, had spent most of his 80 years at the Mission. He was devoted to his only surviving son and spoke proudly of him.

'Albert, him very rich, him Big Boss now,' he would say; but adding that he was sad Albert had left the Mission.

Jonathan died unaware that Albert was no longer 'in the money' and that he had in fact withdrawn from white society in Alice Springs.

Sometimes visitors from overseas went to see the famous aborigine and were shocked to find he lived in a squalid camp. Albert received all visitors courteously enough, but complained of the law which burdened him with all the disadvantages but none of the advantages of citizenship. Dr. Ivar Harries, a Swedish newspaper editor, was one visitor. He watched Namatjira who was sitting on the ground painting, disregarding flies and the dust eddying around him.

Asked if he had any completed paintings, Albert casually pulled one from the hollow of the gum-tree underneath which he was sitting. It was rolled in a grimy cloth.

'Nowhere else I can keep my paintings,' Albert said. 'If it rains, then painting ruined, then hundred guinea lost, gone, finish.'

Albert knew the value of his paintings. The wife of a bank manager in Alice Springs offered him £20 for a painting of Mount Sonder, explaining that this was all she was prepared to pay. Albert did not argue. He simply shook his head.

'You come alonga New South Wales,' he said. 'Do you know Anthony Hordern? Well, you go alonga Anthony Hordern shop. You see Albert Namatjira painting there, him one hundred and twenty-five guineas. Some small, one hundred guineas. Do you say, "Him nice painting, I like him very good, I give twenty quid"? No. Him price you pay what Anthony Hordern say.'

Having made his point, Albert picked up his paintings and strode off. Some time later, the same woman asked Albert to paint a landscape of the Macdonnell Ranges. Albert agreed but demanded 'twenty quid' in advance. She paid and then began to worry whether Albert would deliver the painting. Her husband told her she had been unwise. Next time she saw Albert she reminded him of her order.

'I bring you painting,' Albert promised. 'Me not like bad white man. I be Christian trained alonga Lutheran Mission.'

A few weeks later he delivered the painting. In all his dealings there was never any doubt about his honesty.

In November, 1956, Frank Clune wrote an article, 'Genius in Bondage', which criticized the management of Namatjira's affairs by the Northern Territory Administration. Soon afterwards, Clune set about arranging for Albert to visit Sydney as his guest and to receive a gift of a new utility truck from the Ampol Petroleum Company. He telephoned Canberra for permission for Albert and one of his sons, Keith, to come to Sydney. Canberra advised that an application would have to be made in writing. Subsequently the Director of Native Welfare, Mr. Giese, in Darwin, telephoned Clune expressing his doubt as to the advisability of exposing Namatjira again to the embarrassment of many public engagements. Clune assured him that this would not be the case and that the visit would stimulate the sale of his work. Permission was granted five days later, only a few hours before Albert had been scheduled to leave. Albert and Keith flew south accompanied by Bert Gardiner, an old friend, who was proprietor of an Alice Springs taxi service.

Namatjira had seven crowded days of official functions and engagements in Sydney, including, of course, the presentation of the new utility. This was done on the Ampol Show, the radio programme compered by the late Jack Davey. He was received by the Governor of New South Wales, Sir John Northcott, and met the Police Commissioner, Mr. C. J. Delaney; the Lord Mayor, Alderman Jensen; and Cardinal Gilroy. He was also invited to visit Taronga Park Zoo as the guest of Sir Edward Hallstrom. He went shark-fishing with Jack Davey, called on Father Christmas in a city emporium, and was taken to a variety show. He was also a guest at a cocktail party for athletes who had taken part in the recent Olympic Games in Melbourne and here, as at some other functions he attended, he — and others, too, no doubt — were embarrassed because he could not, by law, drink alcoholic liquor. The only 'dry' occasion was his and Keith's day aboard Jack Davey's luxury cruiser, *Sea Mist*. Davey, always lavish in hospitality and all it implies, ordered the liquor cabinet to be locked for the day out of courtesy to the Namatjiras. The gesture was typical of Davey, one of the best-loved personalities in Australian radio. Albert said later that he had enjoyed that day on Mr. Davey's boat better than any other day in Sydney.

There was also a luncheon arranged in his honour by artists, writers and journalists. Hundreds of people who had gathered to watch the celebrities arrive saw Albert arrive with (now the late) Dame Mary Gilmore, the 91-year-old poetess and 'grand old lady' of Australian literature. Albert gallantly took her arm and escorted her through the crowd and down the stairs into the restaurant. The luncheon was something of an ordeal for Albert. He sat in puzzled silence listening to one speaker after the other eulogizing him and his work in terms he could not comprehend. He just bowed solemnly every time he heard his name spoken.

During his stay in Sydney, Albert sat for the well-known portrait painter, William Dargie.

'When Frank Clune asked me if I would like to paint

Namatjira, I agreed eagerly,' Dargie wrote, 'but as the only free time Albert had from an overwhelming number of social and private engagements was between 5 a.m. and 8 a.m. each day I was a little doubtful. However, Clune said that Albert was always up at five in the morning, so I said that if Albert could get up at 5 o'clock then I could get up then, too, to paint him. So for four consecutive mornings Albert sat for me in a hastily improvised studio in Macleay Street.

'During these sittings I got to know Albert fairly well. I found he was a highly intelligent individual who, if he had been born with a white skin, would have achieved distinction in any sphere. In short, as a portrait painter (and therefore well acquainted with those qualities among white people which lead to distinction among their fellow men) I think I am in a position to say Albert Namatjira was a superior sort of personality — and such personalities, whatever their race or colour, are rare. Albert was a critic as well as an artist, as was proved to me when he said, in regard to a certain well-known Australian painter, "He does not know how to make the side of a tree which is in the light look the same colour as the side of the tree in shadow. If you turn that picture upside down the mountain in the distance would look closer to you than the tree. That is not right. I know how to do it better." These were very painterly observations and I realized I could only regard Albert as a colleague.

'During the four days when I was painting Albert I went with him to several parties and receptions. I very soon saw that he was most unhappy in this strange environment. On one occasion, he came up to me, pushed me in the back and, when I turned around, whispered, "We go now — we go back to your studio and talk about pictures."

'I could not help but compare his attitude to that he had in his own country in Central Australia, where I had accompanied him on painting trips. In his own environment he was so much happier and a most interesting conversationalist. There is no need for me to say what many Australians who have travelled through his painting grounds know to be a

Albert painting during one of his 'walkabouts' in Central Australia

Above   *Albert driving the express buggy across the Finke River, 1923*

Below   *Albert's first house (second from right) which he built in 1926 with local timber and river grass*

Above *Mulga boomerang made by Albert in 1935 depicting the laying of pipes for the Kaporilja Water Scheme at Hermannsburg*

Below *Mulga plaque made and ornamented by Albert in 1932 and presented to Mr. and Mrs. Heinrich as a farewell gift*

The Fleeing Kangaroo painted by Albert in 1935, a year prior to receiving his first art lessons. Reproduced by kind permission of Mr. Oswald Wallent

(Photo: Pastor S. O. Gross)

Above   *Albert building his second house in 1945*

Below   *Albert in a scene from the documentary film* Namatjira the Painter *1946*

(Photo: Department of Information, Canberra)

(Photos: Pastor S. O. Gross)

Above   *Gathering of Aranda Natives after a communion service in the Mission Church, Hermannsburg 1945*

Below   *Albert, with his first truck, prepares to go on a painting 'walkabout' the modern way with his sons Oscar and Enos (1946)*

Left *Albert with his wife Rubina 1947*

(Photos: Pastor S. O. Gross)

Above   *The Namatjira family 1947. Standing left to right Albert, Rubina, Maisie and daughter Rosabelle, Enos, Ewald and Oscar. Sitting Keith and Maurice*

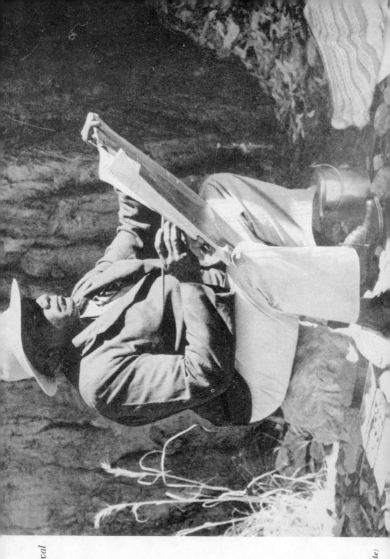

Awaiting the arrival of the Duke and Duchess of Gloucester at Standley Chasm, 1946

(Photo: News, Adelaide)

(Photos: Above — News, Adelaide
Below — Pastor S. O. Gross)

Above   *Ngaire Kunoth (star of the film* Jedda) *straightens Albert's tie prior to his presentation to the Queen at Canberra in 1954*

Below   *Four Namatjira artists—Albert and his sons Enos, Oscar and Ewald (1950)*

Right Canberra 1954.
Albert is presented to
H.M. Queen Elizabeth,
watched by His
Royal Highness the
Duke of Edinburgh.
The Minister for
Territories, the Hon.
Paul Hasluck (who
made the
presentation), and Mrs.
Hasluck are standing
on the left

(Photo: Department of
Information, Canberra)

(Photo: News, Adelaide)

Above A typical scene of the Namatjira Camp in 1954 (Albert
returned to this after his visit to Canberra)

(Photo: News, Adelaide)

Mr. Robert Campbell, Director of the Adelaide National Art Gallery, holds Albert Namatjira's painting which was purchased in 1939. Albert was at the Gallery during his first visit to Adelaide in March 1954

(Photo: News, Adelaide)

Above   *Reg Campbell painting Albert's portrait, Alice Springs, 1954*

Below   *Albert is besieged by autograph hunters in a Sydney store (1956)*

(Photo: Ampol Petroleum Ltd.

Albert shows his
granddaughter
Julianne his
favourite
painting (1956)

(Photo: The
Advertiser, Adelaide)

(Photo: Ampol Petroleum Ltd.)

Above   *The artist and his son Keith, with the late Dame Mary Gilmore and Mr. W. M. Leonard (General Manager of Ampol Petroleum) at a luncheon given in Albert's honour in Sydney, December 1956*

Below   *Albert's last 'house' at Morris Soak near Alice Springs in 1958*

(Photo: Mr. W. J. Pearson)

Above *Albert Namatjira's funeral*

Below *Rubina and the author have afternoon tea together at Hermannsburg Mission in July 1961*

(Photo: Joyce Batty)

(Photo: David Feitz, 1961)

Rubina Namatjira wife of the famous artist and daughter of a ceremonial chief of the Loritja tribe

fact, that Albert was concerned to transcribe as literally as he could, the appearance of his native country. His colours are not exaggerated, except possibly in his earlier pictures when he was learning the techniques of his craft. Albert Namatjira is not, of course, the greatest water colourist Australia has produced, but what he has done could not be despised by any honest painter.'

Dargie found in Namatjira a fine subject for his canvas.

'Albert has tremendous inner dignity,' he said. 'It reminds me of the tranquillity one finds in antique statues, Roman portraits and in the Arabs in the desert. He has the most wonderful face for a portrait I have ever seen.'

His portrait of Namatjira was to win the Archibald Prize for 1956.

And Albert's reaction to Dargie? 'Mr. Dargie, he a clever, fine artist. He paint my face like it's really me. We talk, too, about many things. But not too much. Mr. Dargie don't talk too much like other people.'

Although Albert had been so interested in the way Dargie worked with oils, his only attempt to paint while in Sydney was in the familiar medium of watercolours. He had been asked to paint some city scenes and was taken to Martin Place. Albert set up his easel and with a new box of colours and paint brushes tried to paint the bustling city scene, but, unfamiliarity apart, the noise of the traffic and the curious crowds confused him. He gave up and, exchanging his brushes for a pen, signed autographs for the onlookers. He was besieged by autograph hunters wherever he went and, while he always obliged, he was nevertheless confused by so many people crowding around him. At a city store, he autographed reproductions of his paintings on Christmas cards, but his attitude was one of patient resignation and when he did look up at the mass of faces hemming him in there was bewilderment in his eyes.

Albert seemed bored and very tired whenever he appeared in public and was relieved when the time came for him to return home. His new utility was loaded with many gifts, from a new electric refrigerator to a set of false teeth.

The newspapers in Sydney had made the most of Namatjira's visit and many felt that he had been 'lionized' for the publicity with little regard for his own feelings. The Lord Mayor called for a crusade to improve the black artist's lot and referred to the 'disgraceful treatment' of Namatjira in the Northern Territory.

Bill Harney, a close friend of Namatjira and, at one time, an officer of the Native Affairs Branch, wrote indignantly to *The News*, Adelaide: 'It is unbecoming of the Lord Mayor of a city where citizens of the past had ruthlessly exterminated natives to talk about "disgraceful treatment".'

He added: 'Nothing makes me angrier than the degrading use of a great Australian so that stores might sell a few more of their miserable wares. It seems a shame that Namatjira's fame and ability should be used as a stepping stone by people wanting to glorify themselves. It is only since his work has become fashionable that some people have adopted him. I hope they will be as ready to give practical help when he is an old man wanting support.'

Albert, unaware that once again controversy was raging about him, was on his way back to Central Australia in the new utility, accompanied by Keith and Bert Gardiner, who drove. One overnight stop was at Cootamundra, where Miss Barbara Underhill, the daughter of a former Alice Springs resident, arranged a dinner party in Namatjira's honour.

Hearing that the famous Namatjira was in town, the Mayor hastily decided he would like to welcome him on behalf of the town. The hostess told Namatjira the Mayor was waiting to give him an official welcome. Albert replied: 'All right, send him in.' The address of welcome was read. When it was finished, Albert said to his hostess: 'More lemonade, please, Barbara. Thank you, Mr. Mayor.' And that was that. Albert was never impressed with officialdom. He could like people — but not personages!

During the 2,000-mile journey from Sydney, Albert's pleasure in simple things was apparent.

'Albert saw the illuminated sign of a ram, advertising Golden Fleece petrol,' Bert Gardiner relates. 'He was so taken by this that he immediately insisted he wanted one of those sheep for Biddy, his favourite granddaughter. We already had a full load of gifts for Albert's family, but he continued to insist he wanted a sheep as well. Every time we passed by or stopped at a Golden Fleece station, Albert said, "I'd like one of those sheep." Eventually, at one service station where we stopped, the proprietor overheard Albert's persistent remark and asked me if Albert was serious. "Serious? I'll say he is", I replied. "He has been wanting one of those 'sheep' for the last thousand miles. He has given me no peace for days." The amused but sympathetic proprietor told us there was a discarded "sheep" in reasonable condition in a nearby rubbish dump, deposited there after some local pranksters had removed it from the garage during the last New Year's Eve celebrations, and Albert could have it. With a delighted smile, Albert collected his much-sought-after "sheep", loaded it on the utility and said happily: "Right, now let's get going!"'

Albert's first stop when he got back to Alice Springs was the hospital where Rubina was recovering from an operation. He took in many gifts — bright cotton frocks, pretty scarves and warm blankets in packages which he piled on Rubina's bed.

'When all the excitement of unwrapping the packages was over, Albert personally thanked the Sisters on duty for nursing his wife,' Sister Schneider reported. 'Rubina suggested to Albert that he should paint a picture for both the surgeon and myself in appreciation of our care. A few days later when I was attending to Rubina, she took out of her locker a beautiful painting by Albert and shyly offered it to me, her face beaming with pleasure and pride. When I had thanked Rubina for this lovely gift, I asked if Albert was coming in to see her, and she replied in broken English that he was too busy, "making Christmas still for our people with lots of presents from Sydney".'

And Albert had indeed 'made Christmas' for his many relatives. When he arrived back at his camp, his 30 to 40 tribal relations enthusiastically helped to unload everything from the utility. Never before had there been so many Christmas presents and the excitement lasted for days, children playing with the many toys while their parents ate the contents of tins of luxury foods. Some goods were stored in the new refrigerator which stood useless in the sandy dry creek bed, for Albert's 'home' had no electricity. Albert took little interest in the celebrations. He sat alone mostly in the shade of a gum-tree, thoughtfully watching Biddy playing with the 'sheep' he had brought back for her.

9

IN January, 1957, only a few weeks after Albert's return from Sydney, reports stated that an application had been made for full citizenship rights for him. One newspaper reported that the Lord Mayor of Sydney, Alderman Jensen, had made the application. Another said that Albert himself had applied. This surprised many of Albert's associates in Alice Springs because Albert had several times rejected suggestions that he apply for citizenship. In fact, at one time Albert had sought the advice of a solicitor because he did not want citizenship.

Rex Battarbee was not in favour of full citizenship for his former pupil. *The Advertiser*, Adelaide, reported him as saying that if Albert were granted citizenship, he would no longer be free to roam the aboriginal reserves which provided the subject of much of his painting. A spokesman for Native Affairs, however, refuted this, saying that if Albert became a citizen he would not be prohibited from visiting any reserve where his relatives lived. If he wished to visit a reserve where he had no relatives, then he could obtain permission like any white person.

Pastor Albrecht, who had known Albert for over 30 years, said he was doubtful whether the application for full citizenship had come from Albert himself. Albert had told him that certain people in Sydney had said that he should be a full citizen. Then he could go and live in Sydney and, as a free citizen, would not have to bring any of his large tribal family with him. They would have to stay in the Northern Territory — and he could even have a new wife.

When Albert was asked about the application, he evaded the question, saying only that he could not understand why so much fuss was being made about him.

'All the time people talk a lot about me. Too much talk. That doesn't get me what I want, a house and other things,' said Albert.

Interest in Albert's citizenship ran parallel with discussions about granting full citizenship rights to all full-blood aborigines in the Northern Territory. Meanwhile, the Administration was planning to change the existing Northern Territory Aboriginal Ordinance to a Welfare Ordinance. Under the new regulations, Albert and several other approved aborigines would become citizens.

'Under the existing Northern Territory Aboriginal Ordinance, all aborigines were under the control of the Territory Administration,' the Department of Territories explained. 'The purpose of the Ordinance was to protect aborigines against exploitation. It has always been open to Namatjira to make himself a free man by seeking exemption from the provisions of the Ordinance and the Administration on a number of occasions has invited him to do so. He could have had exemption without delay but always refused to seek one. Under the new Welfare Ordinance, aborigines will not be under the protective provisions of the law unless specifically declared to be wards of the Administration. When the Ordinance comes into force, Namatjira will automatically become a free man with full citizen rights — in spite of himself.'

But Albert had little interest in anything at this time — apart from a commission he had received while in Sydney; the Chairman of the Rio Tinto Mining Company, Mr. Blake Pelley, had asked him for six paintings of the Mary Kathleen Uranium Mine in Queensland. Negotiations for the commission had taken some time as they had to be conducted through the office of the Minister for Territories and the

Administrator of the Northern Territory, Albert being unable to travel beyond the boundaries of the Territory without special permission.

When Rio Tinto was told that Albert could accept the commission and travel to Queensland, an agreement was drawn up, the proposed fee being one hundred guineas for each of the six paintings.

However, in April, before he received the agreement, Albert went to Perth. He was the guest of Mr. and Mrs. Claude Hotchin, at their property, 'Mandalay'. Mr. Hotchin had long been an admirer of Albert's work and had arranged the first Perth exhibition in 1946.

'Albert Namatjira's visit to Perth will always be remembered by everyone who met him,' he said. 'My wife and I found we had never had a more perfect house guest. Albert was meticulous in all his habits, he kept his room neat and tidy and when he used the bathroom, carefully dried the floor after he had a shower.

'We had several long talks with Albert and were deeply touched by his concern for his wife, who had not been well. Albert several times discussed the subject of his citizen rights, saying if he was granted full citizenship he wanted a house in Alice Springs, as both he and Rubina were getting old and living and sleeping in the open was affecting their health. Albert was not well while he was with us: he seemed to feel the cold and my wife provided him with hot water bottles and extra blankets for which he expressed profuse gratitude.

'My most treasured memory of Albert's stay with us was when I found him in his room one evening, sitting on his bed, reading religious verses in a birthday book he had. When I asked what he was reading he said without any embarrassment: "I like the verses in this book, I read them whenever I can."

'Albert spoke of his tribe in most affectionate terms, but expressed doubts about the ultimate results of citizenship rights and the effect on him and his people. He seemed to me to be a very worried and confused man and unhappy about his future. But apart from this, Albert was happy during his stay in Perth. His itinerary was carefully planned to avoid any public demonstrations or publicity that might embarrass him. His engagements included a luncheon at the Rotary Club, a reception by the Trustees of the Perth Museum and Art Gallery, a reception at the Coolbora League attended by many aborigines and part aborigines, a visit to the Kwinana Oil Refinery and a drive around some of Perth's many beauty spots. Albert's delighted interest in any scene that was especially beautiful was proof of his great love for art, as he remarked several times that certain scenes would make good paintings.'

Shortly after he returned to Alice Springs, Albert became a full citizen of the Commonwealth. The popular prediction was that this would be marked by an official function at which he would be presented with his citizenship papers with due ceremony. In fact, when he did become a full citizen, he knew nothing about it until a newspaperman who visited his camp told him.

The statement made earlier, that, under the new Ordinance, Albert would 'automatically become a free man – in spite of himself' is exactly what did happen. When the register of 15,711 full-blooded aboriginal 'wards' was published, Albert's and Rubina's names did not appear. This meant that they were henceforth citizens of the Commonwealth of Australia. Albert could now vote, drink in hotels, take bottled liquor home, build a house anywhere he wanted, and demand the basic wage if he ever worked for an employer.

It all meant very little to him now. He was far more concerned with the Mary Kathleen commission which he had been unable to pursue because of frequent illness and a worrying bronchial infection. In fact, he had not even got around to signing the agreement with Rio Tinto.

Nevertheless, the company made arrangements for Albert to fly to Queensland on 2 May. The Managing Director, Mr. John Poole, flew to Mary Kathleen to meet him. When Albert failed to arrive, Mr. Poole flew back to Melbourne and company executives contacted the Northern Territory Administrator, Mr. J. C. Archer, who had handled arrangements on Albert's side. Mr. Archer found that Albert had gone on a painting expedition with Frank Clune to Glen Helen Gorge, some 160 miles from Alice Springs. Later, Rio Tinto was advised by the Director of Native Welfare that Albert was ill and unable to undertake the proposed commission. The company later made another attempt to have the agreement finalized and the paintings executed. But then it was advised that Albert had had an accident and it would be some time before he could paint again. Since it had already arranged the showing of paintings of Mary Kathleen overseas, the company commissioned another artist.

It was difficult to understand Albert's prevarication since the commission would have meant 600 guineas in fees as well as world publicity. But, as a Native Welfare Officer pointed out, Albert was now free to do just as he wished. Perhaps he was simply making a gesture to show that he was beholden to no man.

By this time Namatjira's fame had extended far beyond Australia and overseas collectors began seeking Namatjiras. A San Francisco man who had seen a reproduction of one of Namatjira's paintings commissioned the captain of a freighter calling at Sydney to buy one for him. Canadians bought sixteen paintings by Namatjira and other artists for 296 guineas. They were exhibited at the Canadian Trade Fair in Vancouver and Winnipeg in August, 1957.

A second film about Albert was made about this time by Norman K. Wallis of Sydney.

'When we arrived at Alice Springs,' Wallis recorded, 'we travelled on to the Gorge, arriving at nightfall, and found Albert and his wife and three sons Ewald, Enos and Oscar, sitting around a camp fire with a number of tribal relatives, shy little piccaninnies and their pet dogs. This was just as I had hoped to find Albert. He greeted us cordially and invited us to share the evening meal of roasted kangaroo and "billy" tea. We sat down on a pile of fresh gum leaves outside Albert's "home", a gunyah that was a makeshift shelter of branches arranged in a semi-circle. A piece of tattered canvas formed a kind of tent. Albert was a good host and told us stories of his boyhood spent around Glen Helen and at Hermannsburg.

' "It is my father's country", he said. "It is my country, too."

'Albert spoke of many things that night. He told us how he saw his country as an artist — the early morning light gently touching Mount Sonder, the blue haze veiling the foothills, gleaming white ghost gums against Glen Helen's red escarpments, the blue waterholes of the Ormiston reflecting the clear blue sky. While Albert talked, his dark eyes gleamed in the flickering light from the flames of the camp fire. His voice softened as he spoke of his father and the sacred myths and legends of the Arandas.

' "He was a flying ant", said Albert, referring to the aborigines' belief that their ancestors were animals or insects or trees, or even stones. "He came flying all the way down from the Macdonnell Ranges, way over from Mount Sonder, way down the Finke River, way down the Ormiston. The 'old men' they tell us these things and I tell my sons. They, too, must know about my father's country."

'But Albert then went on to say sadly that many of the sacred "mysteries" must die with him, as his sons were not tribally worthy of accepting the "big magic" and he did not care to pass it on to those who could not be relied upon to preserve it.

'Albert then told the legend of the dancing girls. In the beginning the Aranda people were all men. There were no women. In the course of time, a tribe of women who lived near what is now called Port Augusta, nearly a thousand miles to the south, heard tell of these fine Aranda men who had no women. So they moved up into the Aranda country, the young girls dancing all the way, dancing along the sharp ridges of the hills and over the mountain crests until they came to Quattatooma and Yapalba, which is Ormiston and

Glen Helen, source of the Finke River. Here they found country they liked and found, too, the Aranda men and they stayed with these men. When these women died, their spirits returned to the crests of the hills over which they danced and took the shapes of trees which can be seen there to this day.'

Wallis said it was easy to believe the legend when one sees the ironwood trees with slender limbs gracefully curved in the fluid movement of a dance.

'We sat with Albert far into the night listening to this elder of the Aranda people telling of this, the country of his forefathers. Albert Namatjira, artist and philosopher, was no mere blackfellow then. He was a poet and a priest, but with the mark of tragedy, for he was the epitome of a dying race, clinging to the remnants of ancient legends and their mysteries.'

Wallis's film, 'My Father's Country', was bought by Ampol Petroleum.

A few weeks after the shooting of the film, Albert, whose health had been poor for some months, went into hospital at Hermannsburg Mission for treatment of a burn on his foot that he had neglected. The Mission people could do nothing with it and sent him to Alice Springs.

The doctor who attended Albert was a recent arrival from England — Dr. P. J. Kerins.

'Having not been long in Australia,' said the doctor, 'I knew very little about the aborigines, but I was fascinated by these dark-skinned people. The dignity, grace and fatalism of the tribal elders intrigued me and the effect modern civilization had on them saddened me. Among my patients in the Native Ward was Albert Namatjira, whom I knew was the world-famed aboriginal artist. On my first meeting with Albert I was deeply impressed and my admiration of him increased daily during the three weeks he spent in hospital. Albert was a model patient. His serenity and obvious confidence in the medical staff was never more evident than when Sister O'Keefe attended him. He was obviously very fond of this

107

amazing Centralian who devoted herself to nursing the native patients. Albert's keen sense of humour intrigued me. My own attempts to cheer up the patients were often only successful when a pithy comment and a deep chuckle from Albert set the whole ward laughing. Usually, however, Albert was reserved. Yet it did not appear that he was overawed by the hospital environment. Rather it seemed that for a time he felt some peace, as if, briefly, he could cease to be the symbol of the battle between two civilizations for the aboriginal soul. I was told that, as a full citizen, Albert had been given the option of treatment in the general wards, but he preferred to go to the native ward.

'As his condition improved, Albert went for walks in the compound. Here, relatives of the patients often camped and Albert's wife, Rubina, saw him almost every day. I asked permission to take some 8 mm. colour movie film of Albert as he talked to Sister O'Keefe in the hospital grounds. He was an excellent subject, above average height, well built, and when he smiled he did so spontaneously without reserve or restraint.

'One day as we walked around the hospital, Albert pointed sadly to a group of aborigines squatting in a circle playing cards. He then said something which, in the light of current rumours, had a sharp significance. He told me he thought gambling was bad, that these men were stupid and that he neither drank alcohol nor gambled. His views were most vehement and they were sincere. I was left with the firm impression that Albert believed alcohol and gambling were essentially evil.

'On one other occasion I was made aware of his strong views. This was in reference to his mode of artistic interpretation. It was while I was saying farewell to him when he promised to give me the first painting he did after leaving hospital. I asked him if he would incorporate his totem in it, but he firmly refused and made it quite clear this was something which his followers did but which he would never do. Later, after I had returned to Darwin, Albert sent me the painting. It was a typical Centralian scene and typical of the genius of a great artist.

'Despite many incidents in my profession, during which I had spent seven years in the Army and two years in Central Europe, the most outstanding was my meeting and knowing Albert Namatjira. I have never met a more impressive character.'

Sister Schneider, who had nursed Rubina, also nursed Albert. She said: 'On admission he was grubby, unshaven and dressed in old clothes that were not very clean, but he fitted into hospital hygiene much more easily than most natives. To those patients in adjoining beds he spoke in Aranda and there was never any indication that he scorned his own people because of his newly-given citizen rights. Albert was conspicuous at meal times by the way in which he handled his knife and fork in a refined manner, while his companions enjoyed eating with their fingers. Although Albert was entitled to be nursed in the white wards because of his citizen rights, he preferred to be with his own people.'

When Albert left hospital, he returned to his camp at Morris Soak. It was rumoured in Alice Springs that he had again tried to buy a house in the town, but without success. In the following months, there was a marked deterioration in Albert's appearance and manner. He looked ill and had aged rapidly. He was sullen, seldom spoke to white acquaintances in the town, and frequently visited the hotels.

Sister Schneider saw Albert several times in the street, but he did not stop to speak, giving only a brief greeting as he passed by.

'I was shocked at the change in Albert,' she said. 'He was showing signs of degradation due to lack of suitable nourishment and the poor quality liquor he was drinking. He mostly rode around in a taxi as his new Dodge utility was often out of order and in a garage for repairs. Some of his sons were selling paintings in the town, including very shoddy efforts by Albert, for as little as £10. It was pathetic to see a fine man like Albert deteriorate in health and character. He seemed to have lost all his self respect and this was tragic.'

Tourists visiting Alice Springs were naturally eager to meet the aborigine whose art had made him the most famous of his race. Mrs. Olga Marks, of Sydney, wrote: 'An American in our party was anxious to meet Albert Namatjira, of whom he had heard much, and whose paintings he admired. Our driver knew Albert well and said, as we stopped near a disorderly assortment of humpies and tattered tents, "Well, this is where Albert lives and, mate, you're lucky, he's home. All we have to do now is see if he will receive you; he is not always 'at home' to white men." We stood and waited outside his humpy surrounded by a group of aborigines, presumably his relatives. After a short conversation Albert got up and slowly, with some hesitation, walked towards us.

'The American was overjoyed when introduced to Albert and shook hands warmly. During the ensuing conversation, I was able to study Albert closely, being careful not to be obvious. His deep bronzed features typified the nobility of his ancestors, a proud race, but the expression on these features was the saddest I have ever seen. While Albert talked, I watched his eyes, twin dark soft velvety eyes in which there was the deep wisdom of his race but also the sadness of his generation. 'Tis said the eyes are the window of the soul and I felt I was looking into the very soul of a great artist, but a tragic man. *Albert Namatjira did not once smile.* Perhaps he would have smiled if more recognition had been given to his people and less attention given to his painting.

'When we finally left Albert and returned to Alice Springs, a perceptible depression settled on us all. No one, not even our voluble American friend, had anything to say. He carefully held two paintings he had bought from Albert and, as we drove away, turned to look back at the squalid camp that was the home of Australia's most renowned aborigine. Probably most of us had the same thoughts. What we had just seen proved the reports we had read from time to time in recent months that Albert Namatjira was an example of a pathetic failure — a failure by modern civilization to adequately provide for the native Australians by means of amenities which they surely deserve and which surely is the duty of responsible Australian citizens.'

10

ALBERT'S citizenship had created a dilemma. Technically, he was no longer an aborigine and, therefore, no longer eligible for protection or assistance provided by the Native Welfare Department. He was entitled to all the privileges of a white man, including being able to live among white people in Alice Springs. But he would not avail himself of these privileges if it meant cutting himself off from his sons, a daughter, his grandchildren and other close relatives. His wife had automatically become a citizen at the same time as Albert, but their children were listed as Wards of the Administration and were not, therefore, allowed to remain in the town after nightfall. The dilemma could not be resolved.

The anomalies of Albert's citizenship continued to provide 'copy' for the Press. Many articles drew attention to the appalling conditions he was living in. Albert's camp had no hygienic amenities. Water had to be transported in containers by taxi. Albert arranged and paid for this. There were reports of drinking at the camp. Published photographs showed empty wine flagons and bottles lying around the refrigerator he had been given in Sydney, its door askew and blown sand in the interior. In the background was the late-model utility with 'ALBERT NAMATJIRA, ARTIST, ALICE SPRINGS' painted on the driver's door, with an acknowledgment that the vehicle was a gift from Ampol.

Albert's failing health affected the quality of his paintings. There were rumours that now he painted only the outlines of landscapes and that other artists completed the paintings. Albert said that he did not always feel like painting these days, but he was under contract to supply a certain number of paintings annually to his Sydney agent, Mr. Brackenreg.

The demand for his paintings continued, and Albert was finding it difficult to fulfil his obligations. Early in 1958 he was again admitted to the Alice Springs Hospital, this time with an injury to his left hand. The bonnet of his truck had fallen on it, lacerating it so badly that the index finger had to be amputated.

Alan Wauchope, who had known Albert for many years, visited him in hospital and reported in *Australasian Post:* 'This is not a story really. It is a portrait made yesterday afternoon in the hot, dusty little road that runs behind the native ward of the Alice Springs Hospital. The central figure is an old man, moustached and bewhiskered, his white hair etched against the still glowing, strong intelligent face—Namatjira the artist. Sitting in a faded pair of blue cotton pyjamas issued by the hospital authorities. Not looking at the glorious hills he had painted so often and so inimitably. Looking at a hand encased in plaster. Sitting in the squatting, relaxed position that typifies his race—in the dust. Resigned. Listless. A long well shaped finger of the right hand traces a little square in the dust. "They want me to paint little pictures now," said Namatjira, the artist. "They tell me that there's not much money in the cities where I sell my pictures. I got to make them smaller and take less money." I thought of Corot's bent tree and the price it commanded at its last sale. I wondered, while Albert looked at his hurt hand, how long he would have to moulder in some Centralian grave before we hear more than ten thousand pounds has been paid for one of his "early works", by some effete collector.'

Malcolm Muggeridge, the controversial British journalist who was in Australia about this time, was also outspoken. He had discovered some 'unpalatable facts'. In an article in

The News, Adelaide, under the heading 'Black Skeletons in Our Cupboards', he wrote: 'Haunting the feast of Australia's prosperity and enterprise are the sad and forlorn lanky figures of the former inhabitants of the country—natives or aborigines and now, by one of those exquisite bureaucratic euphemisms, called "wards".'

Muggeridge could not accept the law regarding aborigines. He failed to see why each State in the Commonwealth had to have separate laws for the aborigines, which debarred them from crossing State borders without special permission.

In July, Mr. Brackenreg visited Albert and spent five weeks investigating his client's affairs. It was then that Brackenreg urged Albert to apply for reversion to 'wardship'. Brackenreg looked into the possibility of building Albert a small pre-cut home on a Commonwealth land grant at Mount Gillen. The *Sun-Herald,* Sydney, quoted Brackenreg as saying that Albert Namatjira and about 30 relatives and hangers-on had recently spent £250 in three days and that 'natives with Namatjira were having wild beer and wine parties at the camp. Whites and half-castes were supplying them with cheap wine and beer at £1 a bottle.' So Brackenreg abandoned any idea of building Albert a house near Alice Springs. He took Albert and some of his sons to Glen Helen Station, where Mr. Bryan Bowman had offered them land for a house, but . . . . 'We had only been there a few days when a pedlar brought some liquor out and they had another party. As a result, permission to build there was withdrawn. It is a tragic situation. If Albert could be left alone away from his relatives he would be quite all right. He was far better off before he was given his citizenship about a year ago.'

Dr. Charles Duguid, President of the Aborigines' Advancement League, said it was high time Namatjira was left alone. Dr. Walter Wearn, a Sydney dentist who knew Albert well and had spent some time with him while making a dental survey of aborigines in Central Australia a year previously, said: 'What right have we to argue what a man does with his family? Albert is a free man. While I was living with his tribe last year I never saw any drinking taking place. Namatjira and his people are living quite happily. I say leave them alone.'

Rex Battarbee came into the picture again with a telephone interview with an Adelaide newspaper. He said that drink was the main problem and that Albert should not be allowed to take it into his camp. Relatives living at the camp shared everything taken there, according to tribal custom, and they were all wards; but the camp was not being policed.

Mr. N. Hargrave, Member for Alice Springs in the Northern Territory Legislative Council, took the matter up with Canberra. In the House he referred to claims that had been made about Namatjira's camp being the scene of drunken orgies because white people and part aborigines were supplying cheap wine at exorbitant prices. The man who had befriended him, now disillusioned, had wiped his hands of him. The Welfare Director, Mr. Giese, had been urged to revoke Namatjira's citizenship and had agreed to an investigation.

The pathetic aborigine in his outback camp became one of the most controversial figures in the country. Pros and cons were argued, often heatedly, sometimes rationally. He became the subject of sermons in churches. Politicians argued that no Australian should ever be deprived of his citizenship. The Aborigines' Advancement League decried the wrong and injustice of Australia's most famous aborigine having no alternative to loyalty to his family except the most squalid living conditions.

And Namatjira himself? 'All this trouble, it make me nervous. I can't sleep. I wish they would leave me alone,' he told a reporter. He had heard that Brackenreg had criticised him in the papers, but he refuted rumours that his business agreement with him had been terminated. 'Not by me, anyway,' said Albert. He understood that his agent held about £1,000 for building a house on land allotted by the Welfare Branch and he would discuss this with the Welfare Office. He was working hard, too. He had been on a painting trip to Glen Helen Gorge, and his agent had gone with him.

He had done nine paintings in five weeks. They were worth £100 each, so why shouldn't he relax with a drink sometimes? But if he had a glass of beer he was criticised. Yet he was only like other artists who like to relax with a drink.

Brackenreg contradicted what Albert had said: 'Albert is mistaken when he talks about £1,000 being held for him to build a house. He doesn't seem to know this money is not his own. It is from the resources of my own company and it was to be a gift to help him build a house. I am still prepared to give him the money if he wants to make a genuine effort to help his people in a community life. But I don't want to see him build a house that will be used for drinking. It is up to Namatjira whether we are finished as artist and agent. I told him he could no longer regard me as his agent if he went on drinking. But I am prepared to go on helping him if he will make the effort. Only two days ago I spoke to our common friend, Rex Battarbee, and I authorised him to select Albert's works. I told him to tell Albert that I wanted to help him. However, I will not pay him money which he is going to squander.' No more was heard of his difference with Namatjira.

Albert continued to live in the camp at Morris Soak. Occasionally he came into town and brought his relatives with him, buying them presents of food and clothing.

It was inevitable, perhaps, that the Lutheran Missionaries who had been his earliest friends and advisers should come under fire for seemingly abandoning him in his troubles. But Pastor Albrecht, who was now resident Missionary in Alice Springs, had, in fact, approached Albert many times seeking to advise and comfort him, but he could no longer get through to him. Albert was bitter and disillusioned, no longer the amiable, courteous man who had won so much respect in the past. On one occasion when he had been drinking he abused Rubina. She came weeping to Pastor Albrecht and begged him to allow her to stay in the aboriginal reserve near the church. She said she would not go with Albert on any more of his painting trips; she was too old to camp in the open and she was very unhappy when the men drank and got rough.

'Albert him bin changed now,' she said unhappily. 'Him often cross and sad. Not like old days on Mission. Everybody happy then.'

Pastor Albrecht, who had bought Albert his first painting materials and had watched with pride the growing talent of the native who would persevere until he had mastered any trade, was distressed by the change in him. Albert curtly rejected the suggestion that he should return to Hermannsburg: 'I am equal to a white man now. I want to live in the town where I conduct my business of selling my paintings.'

When challenged on his reckless spending, he said: 'Why save money? It can't buy me what I want most, a home in the town. They don't want me in the town because of my family. In Sydney people tell me, "Get full citizen rights, Albert, then you live like white man, build home anywhere." But they don't say about my family. What good are my citizen rights? If I drink like I see white man at big parties, I get told off.'

Namatjira's moral and physical deterioration touched the conscience of many white Australians. It was, however, difficult for people in the distant cities to know, still less understand, what the true position was.

But Albert was as incapable of understanding the white man's ways as the white man was of understanding his.

'He often came into the shop where I worked,' a young pharmacist said. 'He was always quietly spoken and, while not very talkative, nevertheless it was easy to hold a conversation with him about his own interests, his paintings, members of his family and his troubles, which worried him a great deal. Albert seemed to have no idea of the value of money; he would buy goods, saying casually, "Book it up." When asked if he wouldn't rather pay cash, he would reply, "All right, mate", as if the thought had not occurred to him and he'd peel off a few notes from a roll with careless nonchalance. Money to Albert was good only for buying food

117

and drink (but not as much alcohol as some reports indicated). As long as his financial affairs were limited to simple matters, he appeared unconcerned. He was either "broke" or "cashed up", two states which followed each other at regular intervals. However, when he was faced with an account for £400 for repairs to his truck, then his whole world seemed to collapse. But when it was pointed out to him that he would only have to do half a dozen paintings and the money from these would pay off the whole amount, life again became simple for Albert. He had a simple method of pricing his paintings. Those with gum trees were £5 more than those without. Bigger paintings were more than small ones and if a prospective purchaser said a painting was not quite up to standard, then he took £5 off the price.

'Albert Namatjira is probably the only Australian artist who looks dignified in ragged clothes, old sandshoes and an old "cowboy" hat which he politely raises when greeting anyone. He maintains a primitive dignity that commands respect. This dignity is primitive not because it is inferior to that of other races, but rather a dignity which is associated with natives in their natural state and which many authorities claim has been taken away from the Australian aborigines following their contact with our civilisation. But dignity, like true virtue, is not dependent on race or creed or social position. Environment may foster or retard it but nothing can totally destroy it in a person who has the strength of character to hold it. And Albert surely holds his dignity.'

But it was already being said that Albert was responsible for the serious alcoholic problem which had arisen at Morris Soak, although he denied that he was taking large quantities of liquor to his camp. He said he knew the law; he took only enough for himself and locked it in an old tin trunk or buried it so that his relatives could not get to it. He blamed a number of half-castes living in the camp who would share their liquor with anyone. The people of Alice Springs predicted serious trouble sooner or later because of drunken brawls that were becoming more frequent.

The situation erupted shockingly when a young woman was murdered at Morris Soak. On 8 August, twenty people from the Morris Soak camp appeared at the inquest as witnesses. Among them was Namatjira. The hearing took five days and many sordid facts were revealed, although the real issue was confused by contradictory accounts. None of the witnesses spoke English well, few understood the long and laboured legal terms of the Court procedure. The husband of the victim was charged with her murder, but in his evidence made statements that involved others. It was clear that some of the natives had been drinking. When Namatjira was called to the witness stand he admitted he had taken liquor to the camp, but said he had not given any of it to the other natives. He had drunk two bottles of beer and some rum, locked the remainder in a tin trunk and then gone to sleep 'because my head wasn't right. I was full. I didn't know anything until I woke up next morning and my son, Enos, tell me about the murder.'

Albert was well and truly back in the national headlines. Douglas Lockwood, who had flown down from Darwin, reported in *The Sydney Morning Herald*: 'Albert walked into the court slowly, shakily, grief in every line of his face. His grey hair was curly and untidy. He looked old and haggard, thin and ill, distressed and shaking. His left hand, from which he had lost a finger, was bandaged. So was his left leg, which he had burnt long ago in a camp fire. The tragedy of all the Australian aborigines was written in his eyes—forlorn, incredibly sad eyes that would have been weeping if set in a white face. But an aboriginal man doesn't cry, especially if he has the stature of an Aranda and the name Namatjira, even if his heart is crying. Standing before the Coroner, Australia's highest paid artist said: "My name is Albert Namatjira. I am an artist." Before he was sworn in the Coroner asked, pointing to the Bible, "Do you know what that book is?" And the Aranda whose ancestors were pagans replied, "Yes, it's the truth." "Do you understand, Mr. Namatjira, what will happen if you don't tell the truth?"

asked the Coroner. "Yes, I will be punished." Albert gave his evidence, listened while it was read back to him, then signed the depositions—Albert Namatjira, the famous signature that appears on pleasant watercolours which hang in homes throughout Australia and in Buckingham Palace and embassies throughout the world. Sergeant Gordon Raabe, who had prosecuted, asked if Albert might be excused from further attendance in the Court, "The witness is ill," said the Sergeant. "You will not need to attend again," the Coroner told Albert. The tragic old man then walked shakily from the Court room.'

Douglas Lockwood said later: 'In my 20 years' experience as a journalist and reporter, I have never witnessed a more deeply moving drama. Albert was a heart-broken old man, bewildered by events for which, so it was implied, he was to blame. I grieved for the fine, handsome man I knew when he was at the height of his fame. Now his spirit was broken.'

Although Albert had been excused from the Court, the Coroner was so concerned by the evidence, particularly that concerning the drinking on the night of the crime, that he ordered Albert to be brought back into the Court. Albert stood with his head bowed as the Coroner said: 'I am very concerned with the drinking orgies that are taking place at your camp. As you are now considered the same as a white man, you will be sentenced to six months' gaol if you are caught supplying liquor to other aborigines who are wards of the State. If you want to drink, you must take it away from your camp and drink alone. I believe liquor in your camp was the indirect cause of the girl's death.'

He then called on Albert to repeat twice before the Court that he would not in future take liquor to his camp.

Albert left the Court accompanied by four of his sons. He stumbled a little as he walked, his worn boots scuffing the red dust beside the road. A taxi took him away, not to Morris Soak, but to Hermannsburg. It was his own idea; he wanted to escape from the misery and humiliation of the past weeks.

It was clear that some solution to Albert's miserable situation had to be found. The Administrator of the Northern Territory, Mr. J. C. Archer, called for the depositions in the murder case. Two well-known Alice Springs people, both former friends of Albert, also gave their views about his future. One of them, Pastor Albrecht, said it appeared that the only solution to his problems was for him to be placed under the Aborigines Act and so again become a ward of the State. Although his citizenship could not be taken away, Albert could still apply for wardship.

Prior to the murder inquest, *The Advertiser,* Adelaide, quoted Rex Battarbee as saying that he and most white people in the Northern Territory were opposed to the granting of citizenship to aborigines, because in the main, citizenship meant only that they could buy liquor. Namatjira had citizenship forced upon him by the Government under pressure from city-bred idealists. Namatjira had foreseen that citizenship would bring suffering and when it had been offered to him 12 months before, he had even engaged a lawyer to appeal against it. Namatjira had not been ready for citizenship. It would be in his own interests and that of his family if citizenship were taken away from him.

But Pastor Doug. Nicholls, the aboriginal clergyman who works indefatigably for the welfare of his people in the Church of Christ Aborigines' Mission, Melbourne, did not agree: 'He (Namatjira) was never given any training for citizenship. Now that he has failed, he is being blamed. Albert's drinking is being used as an argument for taking away his rights and people are using his case as a weapon against full citizenship for all aborigines. The authorities would not let him live in Alice Springs because they were afraid he would lose his culture. The whites have been more interested in his art than in the man himself.'

Dr. Charles Duguid, in Adelaide, said the blame was not all Namatjira's. Albert was an intelligent man and would be able to rebuild his life if given the right kind of help.

'Namatjira has made a name for himself as an artist

throughout the world,' said *The News*, Adelaide. 'In doing so, he has also lifted the world's regard for his people who hitherto have been regarded by majority opinion to be not only primitive but backward. True, as an artist he has proved himself an outstanding member of his race. But what does artistic success mean? Simply that he has a wonderful eye for form and colour and the muscular co-ordination to get it down on canvas. It should certainly not imply that he has any superior claim to wisdom. Van Gogh, Toulouse-Lautrec, Utrillo and Gauguin are among the immortals in the white man's world. Can anyone suggest their modes of life were models of propriety? Or that their neighbours could rightly have been judged by their free-living profligacy? Albert Namatjira is a great artist. As a man, he has his own personal problems. There must be hundreds of Australians who feel a deep personal sympathy for Namatjira now. He has been idolised, pointed out as indicative of what the Australian aborigine could become under strict guidance. His present fall from grace by no means condemns his fellows. Neither does it necessarily mean that he is in permanent eclipse. This tragedy in the life of Albert Namatjira must not be made the reason for any delay in the long-term programme of education and assimilation of the native people of Australia. Rather should it be a spur to much greater efforts to help.'

11

ALTHOUGH Albert was no longer at Morris Soak, the drinking apparently went on unabated. Late in August, 15 natives and three half-castes were charged with drinking while wards of the State. Evidence was given that an elderly woman had been found by police with severe head injuries. The Magistrate, addressing the Court, said: 'I must take a particularly serious view of these offences after the facts that came out at the recent inquest into the death of a young woman at Morris Soak. On that occasion I expressed my concern at the drunken orgies going on at Morris Soak and the violence associated with them. Many of the cases now before me took place in the same area and, moreover, violence evidently took place.'

During the proceedings, the police pointed out that in most cases the natives had been drinking wine. One flagon confiscated was a popular brand with the natives. It was fortified wine with a 23 per cent alcohol content, compared with about 6 per cent in beer.

The alcohol problem appeared to be general among the aborigines. In a case in Campbell, New South Wales, in which an aborigine had broken a bond to abstain from liquor, the Judge said: 'The white man has taken everything from the aborigine and has given him diseases and drink in return. Low-class white men exploited natives by selling them cheap wine whenever they had money. I feel very sorry for the unfortunate man before me. Australia belongs to his people.'

The pathos of the aboriginal people was attracting much attention at this time. Albert Namatjira was accorded particular sympathy. His many admirers hoped he would continue to heed the warning given him regarding the liquor problem. It was generally believed this was so.

Albert seldom came to Alice Springs now. When he did, it was only to buy food supplies to take back to Hermannsburg. But tribal ties are strong. Albert, devoted to his people, would visit them at Morris Soak from time to time, spending the night with them, but always returning to Hermannsburg in a taxi the next day.

Then, on 28 August, Albert was charged with supplying liquor to members of his tribe who were wards of the State. Only the briefest details were released by the police and the Press reported simply that Namatjira had been summoned to appear in Court on 22 September. Even local people knew little more than this.

Albert had engaged a local solicitor, Mr. E. Carter, for his defence. He told an acquaintance in town that he was not worrying. His solicitor 'would settle everything'.

On the morning of 22 September the Court House was crowded for the beginning of the case, but the Magistrate, Mr. J. E. Lemaire, S.M., announced that he proposed to postpone the hearing.

'I called Namatjira to the Bar of this Court and warned him on his drinking habits and expressed my concern at the drinking orgies near his camp,' he told the Court. 'It seems possible that there might be some comment if I sit on this case; in these circumstances my mind might be prejudiced. I can assure you my mind is completely open, but it would be embarrassing for me to adjudicate unless Counsel for both parties clearly asked me to adjudicate. If I am asked, then I would consider it my duty to hear the case, but my personal inclination would be not to sit. There is a rule that justice must be done and not just seem to be done.'

After a troubled silence, Mr. Carter and the Police Prosecutor, Sergeant G. E. Raabe, told Mr. Lemaire they would prefer the hearing to be adjourned. A formal adjournment was then made and the case listed for hearing on 6 October by Mr. S. Dodds, S.M., of Darwin.

The day after the postponement of Albert's case, Mr. Laurie Thomas, the well-known art critic and a former Director of the West Australian Art Gallery, had an article in *The News*, Adelaide, headed: 'Namatjira: The Tragedy Revealed.'

'The tragedy of Australia's blacks has its climax in the tragedy of Albert Namatjira,' Thomas wrote. 'He is the very essence of it. He is torn in half by a conflict no white has had to face. He is neither white nor black, yet he is both. This mad paradox is no mere riddle. It is the stark truth. What is happening to him is as much a tragedy and has almost as much tragic inevitability as what happened to Othello or King Lear or Hamlet. If he fights his way through it and by some stern discipline returns to his former dignity and graciousness, it will be a victory not so much over himself as over circumstances which could break any man. He is trapped less by his own follies—and these have been considerable—than by the demands, the irreconcilable demands of two forces, each terribly powerful and each pulling in the opposite direction. Few white men, and only those closest in contact and sympathy with the aborigines, can have much more than the vaguest clue to the power of the pull of these forces. About 12 months ago, Namatjira was given full citizen rights. He was "made a white man". Before that he was a happy man.

'The point is that a talented, virtuous, highly intelligent man has lost a lot of his friends and perhaps something of himself in the almost impossible attempt to be black and white at once. Namatjira at present looks about twenty years older than he is. He walks and talks with dignity and reserve. But he looks tired and worn out and spiritless. What has brought him to this pass? Whose fault is it? His? Some say so. What is the cause of his present misery? Some say drink. Some say money. Some say too much adulation. Some say weakness. Some say Government laxity. Some say "white" rights. Some say . . . . If you talk to ninety-nine people in Alice Springs you will get one hundred and one different opinions, many of them vehement, passionate, prejudiced. The people in the Welfare Branch have little to say for the simple reason that they have to consult Darwin before they open their mouths. But they will say this. The natives are going through "a transition period". If you ask then "transition to what" they don't know, because although they have plans for educating aborigines in settlements outside towns they don't know how the 16,000 to 20,000 blacks in the Territory will be absorbed in employment even when educated.

'Namatjira is reticent, even shy, with his own dignity. He is one of those with the unbought grace of life. It is certain that he does not speak his whole mind to the white man and it is possible he does not tell all he knows. But there are many people who agree with what he has to say about citizenship. They argue that if blacks had the same rights they would in time find their own level. Most disagree. Some violently. But what has happened and what is happening to Namatjira is to a greater degree happening to the aborigines all over Australia. He is the epitome of Australia's failure to find a formula to translate goodwill into practice. The aborigines are living between two worrying worlds. Here in the heart of the Continent is the heart of the problem.'

The trial of Albert Namatjira began on the morning of 6 October 1958. Hearing of evidence continued throughout the day. Five witnesses were called for the prosecution. They were Constables R. Harvey and G. J. Browning; George Bray, a part-aboriginal taxi driver; Mr. R. D. Kernich, acting manager for Hermannsburg Mission; and Henoch Raberaba, an Aranda artist.

The charge was that on 26 August, during a taxi journey

to Hermannsburg, Albert Namatjira supplied liquor to a fellow tribesman, Henoch Raberaba, who was a ward under the Welfare Ordinance (1953-1957) and therefore prohibited by law from drinking intoxicating liquor.

Albert appeared not to take any interest in the proceedings. He sat with his eyes closed for long periods. Occasionally he glanced up when his solicitor questioned witnesses. Finally, he was called. He rose slowly and walked hesitantly to the stand, where he took the oath. His voice was barely audible as he pleaded: 'Not guilty.'

Albert admitted he had been drinking rum during the journey to Hermannsburg but denied having given rum to Henoch. Albert said several stops had been made during the journey; at the first, Henoch had asked for a drink and Albert had refused him.

'I talk like this: "Henoch Raberaba, I can't give you a drink, of course. You are not right to drink." He told me: "Of course, we should be free citizens all the same we all artists."'

Under cross-examination Albert admitted that he had become intoxicated and that Henoch had also appeared intoxicated. They had an argument over tribal matters about seven miles from Hermannsburg. The taxi was stopped. They got out and when Henoch became aggressive Albert got back into the taxi which drove off without Henoch. A mile further along, Albert said he asked the driver to stop while he buried a dozen bottles of beer and a flagon of wine. He then continued his journey.

Concerning a statement made to Constable Browning on the 28th, Albert said: 'I was sick when the constable questioned me. I understand some place what he asking me, but my head not too good. I couldn't understand all that he said. I can read a little bit some words. Some of them hard words I couldn't read. He write it down when I was talking. He write it down on a typewriter. He asked me to sign that statement. Before I signed it he read it to me. When he read I understand some places. I did not at any time on that trip to Hermannsburg hand the bottle to Henoch Raberaba. I drank out of the bottle myself.'

Cross-examination by the Police Prosecutor followed; then the Magistrate announced an adjournment until next day.

There was a great deal of discussion among those who had listened to the evidence. Much of it, particularly that given by Bray and Raberaba, had been inconsistent. Albert's statements, too, had been contradictory and confusing and, at times, had conflicted with the evidence given by Constable Browning.

Next morning the Court resumed with the hearing of charges alleging that Namatjira had supplied liquor to other aborigines at Hermannsburg. These were dismissed. The Magistrate then gave his findings on the previous day's hearing. Delivering his reasons for judgment, Mr. Dodds read:

1. I find that on the day and at the place alleged, the defendant, Albert Namatjira, supplied Henoch Raberaba with intoxicating liquor, namely rum.

2. I find that the circumstances in which the liquor was supplied were that the defendant and Henoch, together with one Bray, a taxi driver, were together in a taxi en route to the defendant's camp near Hermannsburg. On at least two occasions the taxi stopped and the defendant got out and went into the bushes, leaving a bottle of rum, opened, on the ground or in the taxi. While he was away, Henoch, on each occasion, poured himself a drink of rum and drank it. I point out that I am proceeding on the defendant's version of what happened, and that appears to be the most favourable view I can take of the case. I do not, however, reject the evidence of Henoch. He also says he refused to give Henoch a drink when Henoch asked for it, but admits that Henoch said, 'We should be free citizens all the same we artists.' Henoch is an artist, or says he is. It was after that that the pannikin was given, and

it was after this that the rum was left in an accessible place by the defendant. Even if I were to believe that on the first occasion the rum was left behind it was so left inadvertently—I do not say I believe this, but say even if I were to believe it—I do not believe it was so left a second time. I find that on this occasion at least it was so left in order that Henoch could drink the rum, and, if necessary, the defendant be in a position to say he did not see it drunk. It is straining commonsense too far for me to suggest that I think otherwise. Henoch says he drank half a pannikin of rum the first time and I do not believe any man would not notice that much rum gone from his bottle. It is true that it is suggested that the defendant himself was under the influence, but he was not so much under the influence seven miles from the Mission that he did not notice that Henoch was drunk, and know enough to put Henoch out of the car in an attempt to disassociate himself from Henoch's drunkenness. He was also sober enough to bury his liquor for that time away from the Mission. It is all very well to lean as far as possible in the defendant's favour but, as I have said, there are limits beyond which commonsense cannot be strained. In these circumstances, I must hold, and do hold, that the defendant supplied the rum in the sense that he provided it or furnished it and left it accessible to Henoch. To hold otherwise would be, in my opinion, to mock at proper evidence and to defeat the purpose of the Ordinance. The whole purpose of these particular provisions of the Ordinance is to protect the aborigines against themselves and in such circumstances the word 'supplied' must be construed and applied liberally.

I find that Henoch was a Ward on the day in question. I give full weight to Mr. Carter's submissions on this point, but in my view the averment, at least, overcomes Mr. Carter's objections.

4. I find the liquor was not supplied for medicinal purposes.

5. I find that the defendant knew at the time that Henoch was a Ward.

6. The defendant is convicted.

7. In imposing sentence, I take into consideration the age of the defendant; the fact that at the time his judgment may have been impaired by liquor—there is some evidence that he was drinking in Alice Springs earlier in the day—and the fact that the man supplied was a man of the same race as the defendant. I see no reason in this case why I should impose more than the minimum sentence provided by the Statute. The defendant is sentenced to imprisonment with hard labour for six (6) months.

Mr. Dodds, addressing Albert, said: 'Stand up, Albert. You have been convicted of supplying liquor to Henoch Raberaba by leaving a bottle of rum where he could get it. The least sentence I can impose on you is six months' imprisonment. You were to some extent under the influence of alcohol yourself when this occurred and perhaps your judgment was impaired. I take that and your age into consideration, also the fact that the man you supplied was the same type of man as yourself.'

Albert seemed stunned by the conviction and sentence. He stood for a moment quite motionless, his face expressionless, his eyes half closed. As he was taken into custody he walked slowly from the Courtroom. Outside the door he paused and spoke briefly with his solicitor. Then he was driven in a police utility to the Alice Springs Gaol.

12

ALBERT'S imprisonment aroused a great storm of protest throughout the nation. Adelaide journalist, Ted Smith, described in *The News* an interview with Mrs. Olga Fudge, a part-aboriginal living in the city in her own home, happily assimilated in white society. Mrs. Fudge said: 'No one took the trouble to educate Albert in his new responsibilities, to bridge the gap between being a State ward and a full citizen.' She criticised the people who had taken Albert to the cities only to parade him like a star exhibit in a circus. At public functions arranged for him, he could only speak briefly, but his sponsors spoke at length. This accomplished nothing of value for Albert.

Douglas Lockwood wrote: 'A few years ago, Albert sat in my Darwin home nonchalantly sipping tea and saying, "I don't drink liquor." What caused the change? His drift to drink dates almost exactly from the time he began attending cocktail parties on publicity junkets (not necessarily his own publicity) in capital cities. He acquired the taste for liquor and had no natural resistance.'

In a Press release, the Minister for Territories, Mr. Paul Hasluck, said: 'If anything lies on our conscience it is that at a time when Albert Namatjira was under our protection and was not a citizen, we did not resist strongly enough the pressure from various quarters, doubtless acting in good faith, to take him away from his own environment. Although

131

at that time we sought certain assurances from those who invited him out of the Territory our sad experience was that these assurances were not always honoured. More harm was done to him outside the Territory than anything he learned in the Territory.'

The Victorian Premier, Mr. H. E. Bolte, sent a letter to the Prime Minister in Canberra, seeking clemency for Albert, saying it was his belief that he was expressing the wishes of the Parliament and the people of his State. The Leader of the Opposition, Mr. C. P. Stoneham, supported this. The Premier of Western Australia expressed his opposition to the gaol sentence, saying he thought that 'in this case it should not be put into effect.' In New South Wales, the Premier, Mr. J. J. Cahill, told the Legislative Assembly that he would consider approaching the Federal Government to urge a reduction of the sentence. Mr. P. H. Treatt, a Liberal Member, had asked for this move, saying that harsh treatment of minorities sometimes antagonised world opinion against a whole country as it had done in the United States. In Darwin, the Mayor, Mr. J. W. Lyons, a solicitor, and Mr. R. C. Ward, member for the Darwin in the Northern Territory Legislative Council, criticised the law that had gaoled Namatjira.

Suggestions were made to mitigate Albert's sentence but, before they could be put into effect, the Managing Director of Ampol Petroleum Limited, Mr. W. G. Walkley, suggested that Albert should be allowed to serve his sentence 'confined to barracks' in an approved area within the boundaries of his own tribal country. He offered £2,500 towards the costs on the condition that Albert could continue to paint.

This was followed by a statement by Mr. Hasluck that Namatjira could appeal to the Supreme Court against his sentence, and that the Administrator of the Northern Territory had already informed him that Albert's solicitor was seeking instructions regarding an appeal.

'I want to assure the public, however, in view of the concern that has been expressed, that, if the final outcome should be that Albert Namatjira passes into the custody of the Northern Territory Administration, any sentence passed on him will be served in the open, in his own country and in conditions most likely to help him regain his own grip on life,' Mr. Hasluck said. 'The Administrator of the Northern Territory has already been asked to examine the possible courses of action.'

The offer by Mr. Walkley to contribute towards the expense of Albert's serving a sentence out of gaol was, Mr. Hasluck added, an unnecessary gesture and would not affect any arrangements made. 'While, doubtless, the various offers made for him are well meaning, I think the best hope lies in the influence and help of old and intimate friends in Central Australia and a period of quietness for him, free from publicity.'

Fourteen Melbourne artists sent a petition to Mr. Hasluck. It read: 'As fellow artists and fellow citizens of Albert Namatjira, we wish to express our deep concern at the tragic situation in which he finds himself, a situation not entirely of his own making. We feel that in carrying out the letter of the law a grave injury has been done to his tribal conditions and relationships. Namatjira's humiliation is our humiliation and will already appear so in the eyes of the world. We respectfully and earnestly request that on the grounds of humanity he be released.'

Meanwhile, in Alice Springs, Albert's solicitor had lodged an appeal against both conviction and sentence and the appeal was set for hearing in the Supreme Court in Darwin, probably in November.

Albert was released from the Alice Springs Gaol late on the afternoon of 10 October. He shambled up the long pathway from the prison door which he had entered only three days previously and was driven to his old camping place at Morris Soak.

A Melbourne barrister, Mr. M. J. Ashkanasy, Q.C., was briefed by the Federal Council of the Aborigines' Advancement League to appear for Albert at the appeal.

While waiting, Albert spent most of the time in his camp. He went to Hermannsburg once—to see Rubina, who was now living with a married daughter, Maisie, at the Mission. He tried to persuade Rubina to come and live with him again, but she refused. Hermannsburg held happy memories for her and in her old age she had found contentment there. Indeed, she had been reluctant to leave the Mission when Albert had first left it for Alice Springs; but, like any dutiful wife, she had followed her husband. Morris Soak now held many unhappy memories. Besides, Albert's release from prison might be only temporary.

His wife's refusal to return with him saddened Albert. He packed the few paintings he had done during his stay at the Mission and left for Alice Springs and went straight to a particular pharmacy simply to see Peter Ryan, one of the few people whose company he ever sought during this troubled time. It was a Saturday afternoon. Albert went to the back of shop and found Ryan sunbathing on the lawn.

Concerned about the effect of the fierce sun on his friend's white skin, Albert picked up a shirt, spread it over his bare shoulders and then sat down to talk. Whatever else had changed in him, Albert had not lost his innate consideration for others. Some of the townspeople who had cultivated him when he was at the height of his fame now avoided Albert but he remained loyal to those he trusted and now the sad old man, in need of the solace of companionship, sought it from one of his remaining white friends.

After a delay, the hearing of Albert's appeal began on 15 December. His Counsel, Mr. Ashkanasy, surprised the Court at the outset by announcing that his defence included a writ against the Commonwealth of Australia claiming that the Welfare Ordinance was unconstitutional. This writ had been issued by Enos and Keith Namatjira and Otto Pareroultja, all Arandas, and Claude Emitja, of the Loritja tribe. Its grounds were that the Register of Wards in the Northern Territory had, on 30 May 1957, declared some 15,200 aborigines as Wards without giving any of them the opportunity to appeal and that all those listed had, consequently, been subjected to a change of status and the loss of liberty and proprietary rights. It was claimed, further, that the Ordinance was not a law for the peace, order and good government of the Northern Territory and that the declaration of Wards was null and void as there was no provision for declared Wards to appeal against the declaration. It was apparent that Mr. Ashkanasy, by challenging the validity of the Welfare Ordinance, could challenge the validity of the grounds on which Namatjira's conviction had been based.

The first witness for the defence was Bill Harney, who had lived continuously in the Northern Territory for 47 years and, having married an aboriginal woman, had spent much time with the aborigines. He was regarded as an authority on their laws and traditions. He told the Court he had written seven books dealing with aboriginal life, had been a patrol officer with the Native Administration for eight years, and was a member of the New South Wales Anthropological Society. Questioned by Defence Counsel, Harney told of the complicated tribal relationships and the rigid laws of sharing. He emphasised that the conferring of citizenship on Namatjira did not affect his tribal responsibilities. By tribal law he was still bound to share everything he had with his relations. Harney maintained that Albert's relatives could, by tribal law, demand the sharing of liquor, even though it had been unknown to them until their association with white men. Referring to Albert's addiction to alcohol, Harney claimed that this had begun after his return from an interstate tour. Before that he had never seen him drink.

Albert was next to take the stand. He answered Mr. Ashkanasy's questions without hesitation, but appeared confused when cross-examined by Mr. Withnall for the Crown, on the point of sharing liquor. He explained tribal relationships and said that although Henoch Raberaba was his tribal brother and not his blood brother, he was still obliged to share with him.

Albert, looking very old and tired, resumed his seat behind his Counsel. The court proceedings seemed to weary him. He had taken no interest in the evidence given by his friend, Bill Harney, nor did he wake from his lethargy when Mr. W. McCoy, an acquaintance of long standing, took the stand.

Mr. McCoy was District Welfare Officer of the Native Affairs Branch in Alice Springs. He also had been called to testify on the customs and laws of the Aranda tribe.

Having established the nature of tribal relationships and the tribal law of sharing, Mr. Ashkanasy addressed the Magistrate, vehemently attacking the injustice of the whole-sale unexamined declaration of thousands of native Australians as Wards. The manner in which aboriginal Wards were controlled was contrary to the Declaration of Human Rights for, despite the failure of many white people to maintain certain standards of social behaviour and to handle their affairs, no tests were laid down for *their* qualifications for citizenship.

Giving facts principle for grounds against the conviction of Albert Namatjira, Mr. Ashkanasy claimed that had Henoch Raberaba not been a Ward when, it was alleged, he had been supplied with liquor by Namatjira, no action could have been taken. The challenge to the Welfare Ordinance was reinforced by a document that stated that Henoch Raberaba was declared a Ward of the State without the Administrator of the Northern Territory having had personal knowledge of him; without Raberaba being called upon or invited to show cause why he should not be declared a Ward; and without notice being given that he was going to be declared a Ward.

The main reasons for the appeal against Albert Namatjira's conviction and sentence, Counsel submitted, were that the Magistrate misdirected himself in the law when passing judgment on Namatjira in Alice Springs on 7 October, that the conviction was invalid, that there was no evidence or, alternatively, insufficient evidence to support the conviction, and that Namatjira was not guilty of the charge preferred against him. In the event of all reasons given in the appeal being rejected, Mr. Ashkanasy requested a lesser term of imprisonment or a fine in view of his client's age, state of health, normal manner of living and the fact that there was no record of any previous conviction.

The judgment of Albert Namatjira's appeal was given on 23 December before a small gathering that comprised Albert, his two Counsel, some reporters and fewer than thirty spectators.

The reasons for judgment occupied 36 foolscap pages. In his lengthy examination of the evidence it was apparent that Mr. Justice Kriewaldt had been meticulous. He upheld the validity of the Welfare Ordinance and found that the evidence that Namatjira was, by tribal law, under obligation to share his liquor with his fellow tribesman, Raberaba, had not been substantiated. The eventual summing up of judgment read: 'I think no useful purpose would be served further to indicate the course of my reflections and the problem I have to decide. I must either impose some sentence of imprisonment or a fine of not less than £30. The imposition of a fine is, in the circumstances of this appeal, obviously inappropriate. Giving the mitigating factors peculiar to this case, and the mitigating factors which would be applicable to a white person, also, the fullest weight they deserve in the circumstances of the appellant's offence, I have come to the conclusion that the least period of imprisonment proper to be fixed is a period of three months. The appellant has failed in his appeal against the conviction but has partially succeeded in his appeal against the sentence.'

His Honour stated that in view of Namatjira's Counsel's proposed plan to appeal to the High Court, the decision of the Supreme Court would be stayed to the 15th day after the first sittings of the High Court in Melbourne early in 1959.

13

THE failure of the appeal was a bitter blow to Albert. He had hoped for a complete remission of sentence. Now the strain and tension of waiting would continue. He returned to Alice Springs a free man—but only temporarily, for the threat of eventual imprisonment still hung over him. When he rejoined his relatives at Morris Soak, he no longer felt the urge to paint. He would sit for long periods, staring into space, taking no interest in what was going on around him. He had not only been betrayed by that fickle mistress, Fame; he was now being torn apart by the conflicting laws of his ancestors and white civilisation.

Bryam Mansell, a Sydney artist, found, while on a commissioned tour in India, that the case had been reported there and that many people—including the Prime Minister, Mr. Nehru—attributed it to colour prejudice.

Namatjira, the painter, was almost forgotten; he was now Namatjira, the symbol of the whole aboriginal problem. Throughout Australia controversy increased as distinguished statesmen expressed opinions in the Press. Some supported the granting of full citizenship to all aborigines; others argued that this was neither wise nor practical. The irony was that Namatjira's case supplied both sides with seemingly irrefutable arguments.

In a letter to *The Advertiser*, a council member of the Aborigines' Advancement League, Mr. Barry E. Christophers, wrote: 'As a Christian nation, we must adhere to the fundamental teaching of Christ concerning the brotherhood of man. Christians cannot support laws which deprive a section of the community of their birthright of citizenship. The aborigine is our biological equal and the pharmacological action of alcohol is unaffected by skin colour. Excessive drinking among aborigines is a symptom of their complaint and must not be confused with the disease itself, which is lack of citizenship, low wages and colour prejudices. If Henoch Raberaba, to whom Albert Namatjira is alleged to have supplied liquor, had been a citizen and not a slave then Albert Namatjira would have no charge to answer.'

On the other side, the same newspaper published a joint letter from 13 Territorians—three members of the Legislative Council, a Magistrate, four clergymen and five prominent Alice Springs citizens. It disapproved of 'campaigning for the granting of citizenship for aborigines which, if successful, would do irreparable harm.'

The writers went on to say: 'Citizenship cannot, with any hope of success, be given by enactment. It is our sad experience in the Northern Territory where citizenship has been granted to people of full or mixed blood that, through addiction to liquor and gambling and because the proper preparation was not made, we have on our hands a tragic and growing social problem, with neglected children, deserted wives, malnutrition and vice.'

But the objections were not simply negative. It was urged that before citizenship was granted, all natives should be prepared for it by thorough education, economically, socially and morally. The Government was criticised for failing to provide sufficient opportunity for employment or training for employment. Government settlements on native reserves provided food, clothing and medical facilities but gave little incentive or encouragement to work. Consequently a people once proud and industrious, with strong moral sanctions, were being turned into parasites hanging on the fringes of white society, without proper moral sanctions to guide them.

The granting of citizenship without preparation was tantamount to writing the death warrant of aborigines. It would produce moral decadence which, along with the effects of alcohol and malnutrition, would mean their disappearance in the North, as surely as in the southern areas of Australia.

Dr. Charles Duguid disagreed. With 35 years of experience with Native Welfare and 25 years of close contact with aborigines 'from town dweller to naked tribal nomad' he could argue with authority.

'The greatest factor in the success of the enactment is the attitude of white citizens of Australia,' he wrote. 'Unless the 13 men of Alice Springs and a vast majority of white Australians are prepared to welcome aboriginal people into their homes on an equal footing with their families, legislation will be of little value. The suggestion that aborigines should be "candidates for citizenship in their own land" is a gross insult. Addiction to alcohol is cited as a cause for failure. It is. But what example is being shown to them? If liquor and gambling are to deprive people of citizenship, what an outlook for us all! The statement from Alice Springs avers that present Government policies "turn a race of people formerly proud and industrious in their tribal life (etc.)." That is nothing new. It has happened across Australia ever since people of our race took over tribal lands.'

Dr. Duguid supported the proposal of the Minister for Territories to grant citizenship to all part-aborigines in the Northern Territory.

But Albert's painting was not quite forgotten amid the argument and counter-argument. Indeed, it tended to rouse the supporters of his work to fresh action. The National Gallery in Sydney received many requests to hang a Namatjira painting.

'When Namatjira comes up to standard we will hang one of his pictures,' the Director, Mr. Hal Missingham, replied (*The News*, Adelaide).

Mr. Eric Westbrook, Director of the National Gallery of

Victoria, which had also rejected Namatjira's work, supported Missingham's stand.

'Namatjira's work is just not up to standard,' he said. 'There are twenty or thirty white Australian watercolourists who depict the Australian landscape with greater skill than Namatjira.'

And Mr. Robert Campbell, of Adelaide, also agreed.

'Only the fact that Namatjira is a full-blooded aborigine has caused him to receive so much publicity,' he said. 'Curiosity, not aesthetic value has made him so popular.'

On the other hand, William Dargie, one of Australia's most successful artists, forecast that gallery directors might soon be falling over each other to buy an original Namatjira. He felt that criticism of Albert's work was unfounded and particularly ill-timed, coming, as it did, while he was so deeply troubled.

Noel Counihan, well known as a writer as well as an artist, weighed in with: 'It is disgraceful that Namatjira's work is not represented in all our National Galleries. He has done a remarkable thing. He has bridged a gap of several hundred years between the primitive artist and the modern European painter.'

But the lonely old man at Morris Soak neither knew nor cared that his work was once again the subject of factional wrangling.

On 12 March, in Melbourne, Mr. Ashkanasy, Q.C., applied for leave to appeal against the Supreme Court's prison sentence on the following grounds:

1. That the learned Judge was wrong in law in dismissing the Appeal against the conviction imposed by the Court of Summary Jurisdiction at Alice Springs.

2. That upon the facts before him the learned Judge should have allowed the said Appeal and should have set aside the Order of the said Court of Summary Jurisdiction.

3. That in the exercise of his discretion pursuant to

Section 141 of the Licensing Ordinance of the said Territory the learned Judge should have imposed a fine of not less than £30 in substitution for the sentence imposed by the Court of Summary Jurisdiction.

The Chief Justice, The Right Hon. Sir Owen Dixon, and Justices Sir Edward McTiernan, (the late) Sir Wilfred Fullagar, Sir Frank Kitto and Sir Victor Windeyer were on the bench.

On the day of the hearing of his application to appeal in Melbourne, Albert came in from his tribal country to see his solicitor. After discussions with Mr. Carter, he seemed less despondent. Since the decision of the High Court would not be known until the following day, Albert went to his old camp at Morris Soak, where some of his tribal relatives were still living, to await the High Court decision.

That afternoon the Chief Justice announced that the application for leave to appeal had been refused. All five Judges were unanimous in concluding that Namatjira had supplied liquor to a native Ward, namely Henoch Raberaba.

Referring to number 3 of the grounds for appeal, Sir Owen Dixon said: 'The Learned Judge of the Supreme Court had the advantage of understanding the environment in which the offence was committed and the advantage also of an experience in the administration of the law expressed in section 141 of the Licensing Ordinance. We would be very loath to interfere with the discretion which he exercises in the Northern Territory in estimating what is proper punishment, but in any case we see no ground disclosed by the facts or the circumstances surrounding the offence for doubting that His Honour exercised a proper discretion.'[1]

The Alice Springs correspondent of *The News*, Adelaide, reported Albert's reaction: 'Told that the Full High Court had refused him leave of appeal against his sentence, Albert Namatjira, in an emotional outburst said: "I cannot go on

[1] *Namatjira v. Raabe* (1959) *Australian Law Journal Reports*, Vol. 33, p. 24, *Commonwealth Law Reports*, Vol. 100, p. 664,

like this. I cannot stand it any longer. I would rather put my rifle to my head now and end it all than go on. Why don't they kill us all? That is what they want."

'It was only the reminder that the Minister for Territories had promised that he would serve any sentence imposed in the open country instead of in prison that quietened him. For a long time the artist stood slumped against the stay-pole of his flimsy tent on a barren slope below a rocky hill a few miles out of Alice Springs.

' "Why can't they leave me alone?" he said. "I have nothing now. They have taken everything. They told me I would not have to go to gaol. They told me it would be fixed in Melbourne. What is left for me? I am an old man. I have worked hard. They have taken a lot of my money in taxes, but now I must go and do hard labour." '

It was only a matter of time before he would be arrested and put in custody. The warrant of commitment for the three-month prison sentence issued by the Supreme Court in December had been held in Darwin pending the result of Albert's appeal to the High Court. It was at once airmailed to Alice Springs. Inspector Mackinnon went to Morris Soak and arrested Albert. Albert showed no resentment towards the police officer, whom he had known for 27 years; but, for the Inspector, arresting Albert was one of the most unhappy duties in his long service in the Territory.

Since his first meeting with Albert at Hermannsburg Mission, when he had commissioned the then unknown aborigine to make a dozen ornamental plaques, Inspector Mackinnon had followed Albert's career with interest and admiration. And it had been with genuine sorrow that he had watched Albert's gradual moral and social retrogression.

It was late in the afternoon of 18 March when Inspector Mackinnon delivered his prisoner to the gaol. Precautions were taken to prevent any publicity and not even the towns-people were aware that Albert had been imprisoned. However, the following day this brief communique was issued: 'Namatjira was taken into custody late yesterday on the authority of a Court warrant and committed to prison.'

Although the Minister for Territories, Mr. Hasluck, had said that, for the remainder of his sentence, Namatjira was to be removed to the back country, this was delayed because the place selected was the Areyonga Native Reserve in which mainly Pitjantjaras lived, and a member of the Pitjantjara tribe had threatened his life if he was brought there. The murder of the young Pitjantjara woman at Morris Soak seven months before had inflamed the Pitjantjara and they had sworn to spear any Aranda setting foot on their territory. It was no empty threat and Albert knew it. He begged not to be sent to Areyonga. When the Administrator of the Northern Territory was informed of the situation, he ordered Albert to be sent to Papunya Native Reserve, which was in Aranda country.

This incident was prominently featured in the Press. Albert again became a much discussed figure. The term 'Wanderer Between Two Worlds' was used anew, but now with deeper inference. Albert was described as rejected by two races, his own and that of white Australians; he was also referred to as 'a hapless victim of fate and humanity.'

While most Australians agreed with the decision of the Minister for Territories that Namatjira should serve his prison sentence 'in the open', there was opposition from some politicians, who asserted that political interference with decisions of the Supreme Court and the High Court was insufferable and that it was an incredible state of affairs when a politician could upset the decisions of the most learned Judges in the land. Darwin solicitors went into the matter but could find no section of the Prisons Ordinance or other Act that gave Mr. Hasluck such power.

Mr. Hasluck could not have anticipated such censure of his humanitarian intervention or the Parliamentary debate it provoked. The then Leader of the Opposition in the Federal Parliament, Dr. Evatt, called on Mr. Hasluck to elucidate certain points in regard to Namatjira's 'open' sentence.

144

Mr. Hasluck replied that he had acted to give Namatjira the best possible chance of rehabilitating himself and that, so far from being the worse, he would have a chance of becoming the better for it.

Although some officials continued to object to the special consideration given Albert, humanity prevailed. The Superintendent Gaoler of the Alice Springs prison carried out the order to transfer him to Papunya. Mr. E. L. Fietz, Superintendent of the Papunya Government Reserve, was specially appointed an officer within the Prison Ordinance and became Albert's custodian.

The appointment of Mr. Fietz was in accord with instructions from the Minister for Territories that Albert should be in the care of old and intimate friends who, more than anyone else, could assist with his rehabilitation. Mr. Fietz knew Albert well, having lived at Hermannsburg for a number of years. During 20 years as a schoolmistress at Hermannsburg, Mrs. Fietz had also become a close friend of the Namatjira family.

During the few days Albert had spent in Alice Springs gaol, a doctor examined him and found high blood pressure and an enlarged heart. He recommended that Albert be given only light duties. The original court order was hard labour, but gaol officials made every effort to ensure Albert's wellbeing. His light duties were preparing vegetables for meals and sweeping paths around the lawns and flower beds in the prison compound. Albert went through his duties like an automaton. He spoke only when spoken to, answering in monosyllables. He was apathetic and aged beyond his years. It seemed that, with his ingrained aboriginal fatalism, he had resigned himself to the condition that cruel circumstances had created.

When he went to the gaol to take Albert to Papunya, Mr. Fietz saw at once that Albert was quite indifferent to what was happening to him.

14

A T Papunya, special security measures were introduced for the term of Albert's sentence. Members of the staff could not talk to him and he was segregated from the other 600 aborigines on the settlement. Visitors were banned and cameras prohibited. Mr. Fietz was instructed to house Albert in suitable quarters, provide him with three meals a day and keep him under constant surveillance, but Mr. Fietz combined the carrying out of orders with friendship.

Albert had seemed apprehensive when he arrived at Papunya. Mr. and Mrs. Fietz did their best to dispel his misgivings. They took him into their home for tea. But if Albert appreciated the gesture he did not show it. His face was an inscrutable mask, his dark eyes devoid of expression.

The Fietzes were greatly troubled by Albert's attitude and appearance. It was difficult to relate this stooped, haggard old man with the Albert they had known at Hermannsburg — the happy husband and proud father, the honoured tribesman of the Arandas, a respected member of the Mission community. He appeared to have lost interest in everything. Mr. Fietz suggested he should share the family meals but Albert refused, preferring to eat outside, sitting in the shade.

Fietz then suggested that Albert come along when he made routine inspections around the reserve. Albert agreed, but without enthusiasm. Nevertheless, this was the start of the break-through. As they drove through country rich in the legends of his people, nostalgia for his childhood began to break down Albert's barrier of indifference. For the first time since coming to Papunya, he talked voluntarily. He recalled the tribal legends associated with each landmark — legends he had learned from his father, legends of the Dreamtime when the mighty totem heroes had created the mountains, ravines and rock pools. He told of the prowess of his tribe in great battles and the feasts that followed and the corroborees of victory which his father had participated in before the coming of the Christian missionaries.

He began to talk more freely with the Fietzes and some of the warmth of their old friendship returned. The four young Fietz children often sat with Albert while he ate his meals. Their company seemed to please him and he would smile at their behaviour. His natural dignity returned and with it a renewed confidence in human goodness. He began reading his Bible and hymn book again — both printed in Aranda — and seemed to derive comfort from the religion he had abandoned during the troubled years leading to his conviction.

The Superintendent Gaoler from Alice Springs, accompanied by the Welfare Officer and the Director of Native Welfare, visited Papunya regularly as a matter of routine. They realised how beneficial was Albert's 'open' detention, even though he seemed a little apprehensive in their presence — no doubt because they were reminders of his troubles. He told Fietz he knew drink was bad for him and asserted that he would never again touch intoxicating liquor.

While driving around the reserve with his custodian, Albert began to tell more and more about his life. He spoke of the big cities and confessed that he did not enjoy them. He particularly disliked his stays in Sydney, where he had been rushed from one function to another and had always been surrounded by curious crowds. Few seemed to care about him as a person. He said that at Papunya he had found peace and if he could stay there after his sentence had been served he might, in time, find the heart to paint again.

But he had one heartache at Papunya. He wanted to see Rubina. The Fietzes had been worried about the rift in Albert's marriage so they arranged for Rubina to visit Papunya — Albert was allowed two visitors a fortnight. Husband and wife were reconciled and, as there was no law prohibiting her from living on the Reserve, she would have stayed. But when she was told she could not visit the place of Albert's detention except when regulations permitted, she broke down and wept. Only the assurances of the Fietzes that Albert would soon be released comforted her. Sobbing, she took leave of her husband and returned to Hermannsburg.

Apart from this unhappy scene, Albert lived from day to day, free from disturbing conflicts. For six weeks his name did not once appear in the newspapers, although a strange aircraft seen circling low over Papunya was believed to have been chartered by a hopeful Press photographer.

Then, in a tribal fight at Papunya, two natives were killed and many injured. It was hinted by some papers that it had to do with threats made against Namatjira by the Pitjantjara tribe. In view of the wild accounts of the incident, Mr. J. N. Nelson, the Labour member for the Northern Territory, asked for an official statement from the Minister for Territories. Mr. Hasluck deplored the highly coloured and often inaccurate reports. He said that when they had first appeared, he made strenuous efforts to 'correct that fiction' and present the facts, but although some newspapers responded, there were others that seemed to apply the principle that you should not spoil a good story by telling the truth.[1] The disturbance had been simply a tribal dispute among members of the Pintubi tribe and was not even remotely connected with Namatjira who was, at the time, with the Manager, Mr. Fietz, on an inspection tour of Haast's Bluff.

Because of the often unsavoury publicity that would envelop Namatjira on any pretext, as the completion of his sentence approached precautions were taken to ensure that no information about him percolated outside. He was granted

[1] Extract from Hansard Question, 5 May 1959.

full remission for good behaviour—which meant his three-month sentence was shortened by one month. The date set for his release was 18 May. Details of his release arrangements were transmitted over the Royal Flying Doctor Service radio by a code previously agreed between the Superintendent Gaoler at Alice Springs and Fietz.

Albert's formal discharge would be from the Alice Springs Gaol, so he had to be driven to town. Fietz called in at Hermannsburg to send a radio message to the Gaol. Although Rubina had not been told that Albert would be passing through, she recognized the Papunya truck and then saw Albert in the cab. She ran to greet him and was overcome with emotion. Clinging to Fietz's hand she murmured her tearful gratitude for bringing Albert back to her. It was difficult for him to explain that Albert was not yet free, that he had to go to Alice Springs to be officially released and that then he would be free to return to Hermannsburg. Rubina wanted to go to Alice Springs to be with Albert when he came out of gaol. Fietz assured her that he would arrange it with the Mission Superintendent. Then he and Albert continued their journey.

Rubina stood watching the dusty road long after the truck had disappeared from view. The loneliness and unhappiness of the past year were almost at an end. With the faithfulness characteristic of aboriginal women, she had waited. Now she would begin a new life with her man. During their 38 years of marriage neither poverty nor famine nor sickness nor the loss of four of their children had affected the unity of Rubina and Albert. But where adversity had failed, the white man's civilization succeeded. Albert had lost his way in the unaccustomed power of money and the adulation of the big cities. He had been confused by customs he did not understand. Rubina had had none of Albert's close contact with white civilization, but she had no illusions about the 'privilege' of belonging to it. Full citizenship had brought only an accumulation of unhappiness. Instead of being elevated to a better way of living, Rubina and Albert had been ground down by laws which neither understood. Now there was hope. Rubina knew Albert had been well and wisely cared for in the custody of their old and trusted friends at Papunya and that he had benefited from their influence. She knew also that he would now return to his own country and that there they might again find peace and happiness in their closing years.

On the morning of 19 May, Albert walked out of the high-walled Alice Springs Gaol. At the gateway he was met by his wife and members of his family who were waiting to take him back to Hermannsburg, but Albert said he had business to attend to in the town first. He asked to be driven to his taxation adviser, Mr. Owen. There he left his family, telling them he would take a taxi back to the Mission.

Owen, unaware of Albert's release, was surprised to see him and even more surprised when he said he had called to discuss certain business problems; for Albert had taken little interest in business matters, invariably dismissing any problem with: 'You fix it, Mr. Owen. I don't worry.'

Albert had always been casual, always vague about his income, the number of paintings sold, his agent's commission and similar details which interest the Commissioner of Taxation. Now he seemed anxious to get his affairs in order. He wanted to clear up an enquiry from the Taxation Department about variations in agents' fees, which did not tally. Another problem was the large amount owing for repairs to his truck. He said he must pay this account, but did not have the money since he had not earned anything for some time. He was also concerned over the contract with his Sydney agent whereby he was required to supply a specific number of pictures annually.

'Even before my prison sentence, I not always feel like painting,' Albert explained wearily. 'Got to be in the mood. Can't turn out paintings like machine. These no good.'

Owen suggested he might now feel like painting again.

'I can't paint yet,' Albert said. 'Still too sad. When I live with my own people again, in my own country, perhaps then I paint.'

Asked if he had decided where to live, Albert replied that he had been offered a cottage at Papunya, but was not yet sure if he would accept.

'First I go to Hermannsburg,' he said. 'I go back to my father's country. It's my country, too. Can't be happy anywhere else now.'

Looking at the sad old aborigine, Owen was reminded of the last lines of Sir Walter Scott's 'Lay of the Last Minstrel':

> Land of my sires! What mortal hand
> Can e'er untie that filial band
> That knits me to thy rugged strand!

Albert suddenly arose, held out his hand and, with a brief farewell, left. His abrupt departure startled Owen, who hurried to the door with misgivings he could not define. He returned to his office where one of Albert's earliest paintings hung on the wall. He had often regretted not buying a later work painted when Albert's skill was at its peak. But the small painting had more than sentimental value; the simplicity of line and soft pastel colours might not have the confidence of his later work but it did reveal a love of painting for its own sake and not for the sake of money to pay his debts.

Meanwhile, Albert called on another friend, Mr. Reg Verran, who had for some time despatched some of his paintings to his agent in Sydney. He, too, was surprised by Albert's unwonted interest in his business affairs. Albert told him he wanted to know just how many paintings had been sold in Sydney and was urgent in his insistence that his affairs be settled. He gave the impression that he was not interested in making plans for the future. Albert summoned a taxi and left for Hermannsburg. Verran, watching the taxi drive away, had an uneasy feeling that he would never see the old man again.

Albert's strange manner which had left his two white friends with a vague foreboding was also noticed by his family and the Superintendent of the Mission. In the days following his return to his old home, Albert resisted the efforts by his family and Pastor Scherer to interest him in taking up some activity. He seemed content to sit outside the hut he shared with Rubina. At length he agreed to Pastor Scherer's suggestion that he should accept the offer of a cottage at Papunya.

At Papunya, the Fietzes made Albert and Rubina as comfortable as possible in their new home. Rubina was particularly grateful, but Albert, still possessed by lethargy, seemed to prefer his own company, spending most of the time sitting alone, gazing for hours at a time across the landscape. After a time he did show signs of a revival of interest in painting. He would start a picture, then drift into a trance-like state and not add another brush stroke all day. Then he would watch the sun set, the purple mountains casting their lengthening shadows across the red plains. The sudden chill wind off the desert and the swiftly winging birds seeking shelter for the night would stir him from his reverie. Gathering up his unfinished painting, his colours and brushes he would trudge back to the cottage.

Albert's continued lethargy perturbed Fietz. He hoped that a discussion about his painting might stimulate him. One day he approached Albert as he sat alone and asked if he had completed any paintings. Without comment, Albert took several watercolours from a bag by his side. They showed almost startling evidence of the turmoil in the old man's mind, with harsh, almost aggressive colours. The instinctive keen observation of the landscape was still apparent in the contours of the towering ranges and the graceful white-limbed ghost gums; but there was none of the sense of colour that had characterized his early work.

Fietz was disturbed by these paintings. He handed them back to Albert, hardly knowing what to say. After a moment, he asked Albert what he intended to do with them. Albert thought he might give them to Enos to take to Battarbee, but his tone indicated that he did not really care what became of them.

Albert appeared to have lost the will to live. On several occasions, Fietz asked him if he was worried about anything or if he felt ill. Invariably Albert replied that he was all right, just felt a little bit tired. When Rubina was called to Hermannsburg to look after Maisie, who was due to have a baby, she asked the Fietzes to take care of Albert. They assured Rubina they would and asked Albert to have his meals with them; but Albert refused. Several days later, Mr. Fietz, on his rounds, found him huddled in a corner. Albert complained of pains in his chest.

Fietz immediately called the two Sisters in from the Papunya Hospital. Albert seemed to resent their examination but, knowing his medical record of angina, they insisted. Although they found nothing to cause immediate alarm, they suggested that Albert come to the hospital. Albert refused. Mr. Fietz asked one of the Sisters to contact a doctor at Alice Springs during the next radio session. The doctor on duty, also aware of Albert's medical history, advised a close watch on his condition and asked that any change be reported. During the next two days Albert's condition showed no improvement. The doctor suggested sending a plane to Papunya to fly him to Alice Springs. But Papunya did not regard Albert's illness as serious or urgent, so it was decided to send him to town in the truck when it went for supplies. The Sisters and Mr. Fietz made Albert comfortable on a mattress in the back of the truck.

Albert insisted on sitting up and waved as he was driven away. Although he seemed in reasonable condition, Mr. Fietz began to worry that the long journey might have a bad effect on him, so he had a radio message sent to Alice Springs asking for an ambulance to be sent to meet Albert. A few hours later Papunya heard by radio of Albert's safe arrival at hospital. His condition? Satisfactory.

Albert rested the next day. Then without warning, he had a heart attack. His condition deteriorated rapidly and became critical with the onset of pneumonia. Rubina was told and a Mission vehicle brought her to the hospital the following afternoon. Here Pastor Albrecht met her and together they went to Albert. Kneeling by his bed, they prayed and Albert, making a great effort, joined them in the Lord's Prayer. With a faintly whispered 'Amen', he wearily closed his eyes and lapsed into a semi-coma.

As the last glow of sunset cast soft shadows across his dark face, Albert sighed deeply. The Aranda tribesman who became Australia's most famous and most tragic artist was dead.

Albert Namatjira was buried in the Alice Springs cemetery late in the afternoon of Sunday, 9 August. The burial service was simple and brief in deference to Rubina and her grieving family.

Pastor Albrecht, robed in the long black surplice of his office, first offered prayers in Aranda, then made a short address based on the text, 'By the grace of God, I am what I am.' He said: 'Albert, as we called him, was not only a member of the Aranda tribe and of the Lutheran Church; I venture to say he was not looked upon as belonging to Australia only. He was a world figure. Through his art he had interpreted the beauty of this country to a vast multitude of people. He made them see our ranges, trees and landscapes in that glorious sunshine that perhaps no other corner of the globe knows of. And today we are to commit his remains to the earth of God. But, praise God, we are not laying all of the great son of Central Australia to rest here; there is much that will remain with us. In countless homes of this country, his paintings will continue to delight the hearts of people.'

As the service ended, Rubina, carrying a small bunch of flowers, came forward, led by Pastor Scherer. Together they cast the first earth on the lowered casket. High above the grieving mourners a solitary glider soared silently in slow wide circles. As the winged shadow passed over the open grave, it was as if, symbolically, the anguished spirit of Albert Namatjira was released from the tribulations of his earthly life, at last freed to seek the places of happy memories and there finding lasting peace.

Only a few local people remained as Albert's grave was covered with flowers. There were elaborate tributes from eminent public figures throughout Australia alongside small posies from friends and admirers.

But Albert could not even be buried without provoking controversy. Many felt he should have been honoured with a civic funeral. There was also objection to his being buried in Alice Springs because it was not in Aranda territory and had been the scene of Albert's miserable dissolution. Pastor Albrecht retorted that Albert's funeral arrangements had been in accordance with Rubina's wishes and he, personally, felt that a large public funeral with many strangers present would have embarrassed the Namatjira family.

But Albert's passing was, nevertheless, mourned far beyond the little cemetery in Central Australia.

Doctor Evatt, Leader of the Federal Opposition, said: 'Albert Namatjira's death is a tragic loss, not only to his own people, but to all Australia. What he helped greatly to do was to bring together in true sympathy the Australian native peoples with all of us.'

Sir Hans Heysen, one of Namatjira's earliest admirers, said: 'In his own way, Albert was unique. His power of observation was remarkable. Pastor Albrecht sought my advice on what should be done with Albert and I advised that this talented aborigine who, in those early days, showed great promise as an artist, should be left in his own country to paint what he felt. Unhappily that was not done.'

Emeritus Professor A. P. Elkin said that Namatjira's death was a serious loss to the aborigines because he was a great leader of his race: 'I only hope that the enthusiasm shown for Albert's accomplishments will not wane with his death.'

William Dobell, one of Australia's greatest artists, said: 'I am sorry to hear of Albert's passing. I admired him as a man and as an artist.'

Author Frank Clune, host to Albert when he visited Sydney, said: 'Poor Albert . . . he was the most outstanding aborigine this country has produced. He had the bone pointed at him and he died of a broken heart. He should be buried alongside John Flynn in the shadow of Mount Gillen.'

Dr. Charles Duguid, always a champion of Albert's in controversy, said: 'I have known Albert since 1934 and have always held him in high regard. As well as an artist, he had a great mind. He could discuss Australian affairs like a well-informed white man and he was greatly under-estimated.'

Mr. Gordon Simpson, who had known Albert for 19 years and who owns one of the largest collections of his paintings, said: 'I knew Albert well and had a great regard for him. I consider him the greatest painter ever to paint the Northern Territory. His work showed an immense depth of feeling for his country, a feeling no white man could portray. As a family man he was devoted to his wife and children. He will be sadly missed by them all. He was a man of very high ideals. He had set ideas, but could converse with anyone from any walk of life.'

Artist Noel Counihan, an admirer of Albert Namatjira, attempted an assessment of his achievement. In an article in *Tribune* he deplored Namatjira's rejection by official and professional art circles and his social rejection when he attempted to make his home in Alice Springs.

'National Gallery directors, lecturers on art, critics and many well-known painters have stated that Namatjira's work has little artistic merit,' he wrote. 'Sydney Gallery director, Hal Missingham, said publicly that he considered there were 25 water colourists in Australia better than Namatjira. I am waiting for him to name them. Sir Daryl Lindsay refused to purchase Namatjira's watercolours for the Melbourne Gallery when he was director. Namatjira's place in our art must be seen historically in its exceptional circumstances. It is a disgrace that our major National Galleries have ignored him, but in spite of this, the common people, the broad lay public, loved Namatjira's warm, colourful paintings. He rose to fame with nothing but his natural abilities. He had no cultural tradition by which to establish values. Great artists do not rise from a vacuum. Behind Rembrandt lay two centuries of richly developing realist art in the magnificent Dutch tradition. Rembrandt was familiar with and owned examples of the greatest Italian art of his day. These are the familiar circumstances which throw up great figures. Yet Namatjira was a great artist. He possessed an absolutely unique gift in addition to a painter's eye, keenly sensitive to colour, a vivid memory, a formidable intelligence and a warm love for his country. He took a vast cultural leap spanning thousands of years. He opened up a rich vein of talent in his own people, laying the base for a regional school of Aranda painters.

'Irrevocably, he made his own contribution to our national tradition. Yet he was rejected because of the realistic challenge he presented to an art world engaged in a wild flight from reality. In abstract art, the rejection of reality is complete. The fundamental values of art have been turned upside down. What is ugly is called beautiful, the formless is praised for its strength, the empty considered profound. Namatjira aroused much prejudice and hostility in the professional art world by his successful invasion of the white man's market. But history and posterity will give Namatjira the honourable place in our art to which he is entitled.'

One of Australia's foremost journalists, Clive Turnbull, wrote in a feature in *The Sun*, Melbourne: 'The lamentable truth is that most of us feel that something should be done about the aborigines but only the very exceptional citizens do anything at all. Our agitation about Little Rock or Nyasaland is not much more than hypocrisy. Condemnation of the sins of others will neither gild nor palliate our own offences. It is hurtful, if only to our own vanity, to think that we belong to a generation which our successors will condemn not only as heartless but as lacking in the rudiments of civilization in our attitude to the aborigines. We cannot even trump up the excuses that may be made for our own ancestors or for the conquistadores. We are all guilty and, if our critics were to say we couldn't care less, we should have a hard job to disprove the assertion.'

Some Australian newspapers devoted editorials to him.

The Advertiser, Adelaide, said: 'A significant aspect of Namatjira's life and work is that he helped make us more self critical, even censorious, of our attitude towards aborigines. Probably more than anyone else he stirred the community's conscience in this matter. In helping create interest in his country, his eagerly sought paintings often provided more effective publicity than whole departments and his cultural achievements sharpened our awareness that the conditions of aborigines should be improved and their status raised. Of dignified and even handsome appearance, the Aranda artist became an influential though unofficial ambassador for his race.'

As well as extensive tributes by Australians, Albert Namatjira's death was also reported widely abroad. He was even known as far afield as Russia, although his work was known only through reproductions. In England, *The Times* gave Albert pride of place in its obituary column, referring to his primitive background, education at the Hermannsburg Lutheran Mission, his first painting lessons and subsequent success which had merited Royal patronage.

The final tributes collectively inscribe the last chapter in the life of Albert Namatjira. A singular tribute by Leonard J. Flynn appropriately closes this chapter.

Sleep on, gentle soul, your resting place not
*   marked by pillared stone*
Your black clay now inblended with the reds and browns
*   of the great land your tribe once called its own;*
Blank now the visionary eye that saw beauty in a stone
*   or stunted tree;*
Stilled now the mind once filled with tribal law,
*   the legends old, the mystic wild corroboree.*
The generous heart, the helping hand, has left
*   a memory sublime;*
No need have you for epitaph, you've left your brush work
*   on the canvas of our time.*

(*Epitaph* by Leonard J. Flynn (1959). Reprinted by kind permission.)